THE
MAGPIE EFFECT

THE

MAGPIE

EFFECT

Your complete and comprehensive guide
to surviving and enjoying the twisted
social media era. #UnsocialMedia

DAMIEN MASSIAS

Matador
9 Priory Business Park,
Wistow Road, Kibworth Beauchamp,
Leicestershire. LE8 0RX
Tel: 0116 279 2299
Email: books@troubador.co.uk
Web: www.troubador.co.uk/matador
Twitter: @matadorbooks

ISBN 978 1789017 274

British Library Cataloguing in Publication Data.
A catalogue record for this book is available from the British Library.

Printed on FSC accredited paper
Printed and bound in Great Britain by 4edge Limited
Typeset in 11pt Minion Pro by Troubador Publishing Ltd, Leicester, UK

Matador is an imprint of Troubador Publishing Ltd

The Crow and The Fox
By Jean de La Fontaine

Master Crow sat on a tree,
Holding a cheese in his beak.
Master Fox was attracted by the odour,
And tried to attract him thus.
"Mister Crow, good day to you.
You are a handsome and good looking bird!
In truth, if your song is as beautiful as your plumage,
You are the Phoenix of this forest."
Hearing these words the Crow felt great joy,
And to demonstrate his beautiful voice,
He opened his mouth wide and let drop his prey.
The Fox seized it and said: "My good Sir,
Know that every flatterer,
Lives at the expense of those who take him seriously:
This is a lesson that is worth a cheese no doubt."
The Crow, embarrassed and confused,
Swore, though somewhat later, that he would never be
tricked thus again.

Contents

Why
"The Magpie Effect"?

I was once with my dad at his home in the French countryside in the middle of nowhere, and we saw a magpie, a bird indigenous to that area. He told me that magpies love everything that shines, and they're considered to be one of the most intelligent birds since they're one of the only non-mammal species with the ability to recognise itself in a mirror test.

When I decided to write my book, the image of that magpie immediately came to mind as I realised us social media users remind me somewhat of magpies. We're attracted to our shiny devices, shiny apps on our screens, shiny accounts, shiny people and everything shiny beyond. To boot, we're quicker than ever to recognise, obsess over, and share our own reflections *on* social media. A Google search would yield an entirely different meaning of "the magpie effect," but for me, for this book, it is just about how dazzled we are by the shiny social media surrounding us.

I wish you a wonderful read.

Introduction

Some people are passionate about sports. They know every team, every stat, every rule well enough to predict winners and losers, and spot connections and trends throughout the seasons. My passion? People. And if you were to categorise the many elements of human behaviour into teams, stats, and rules, I'd be the one passionately rattling them off.

My name is Damien Massias. I am a life coach, specialising in two areas: mindset and confidence, and dating and relationships. For the last 15 years, I've lived my professional life as some sort of modern philosopher—constantly questioning, analysing, and dissecting society and people's patterns, habits, achievements, downfalls, and beyond. My father himself was a coach for unemployed people, helping them to gain the necessary confidence for job interviews and other opportunities to turn their lives around. With just under 10,000 books in his library as I grew up, I'd call him a "philosopher" too. My stepmom was a child behavioural expert. So I was born into a family of people who were constantly wondering about... well, *other* people. My father instilled in me a curiosity to expose the *whys* and *hows* of what's happening around us. As a child, I overheard many a discussion about my parents' clients, the common denominators among them, and their shared recurring patterns despite these people seeming totally different on paper.

Trust me, as a kid, it wasn't all that fun! Or maybe I should rather say: it didn't strike me as important or interesting. When you're younger, you don't see the bigger picture. The things your parents say go in one ear and out the other! However, I guess without realising it, growing up in that environment did indeed have a lasting impact on me. As I grew up, I too became very interested in trying to find out, help, compare, solve "life puzzles." So when it came to the beginning of my professional life, I set out on a life long quest, full of curiosity, awareness, a genuine love and care for people, an ever-growing collection of tools, and a thirst to really *understand*.

This introduction isn't meant to be a CV. I have no intention of listing out my qualifications for you wise readers to deem me "qualified" enough to read this book. However, I think it would be interesting for you to know about a few different parts of my life that contributed invaluable insight to the conclusions drawn in this book. And these experiences are ones you *wouldn't* find on a CV, yet they're the ones I consider to have been most influential of all.

1) I was a lifeguard.

My first job ever was as a summer lifeguard in the south of France. I was the youngest one by about 25 years and though the pay wasn't great, I quickly became rich in emotional intelligence by listening to the stories of my much older colleagues. I learned about their relationships, regrets, doubts, fears, and victories. We discussed the things kids my age certainly wouldn't be discussing for another few years. That summer, a seed took root: a deep respect for those older than me, and a reverence for everything I could possibly learn from their experiences.

I then worked as a lifeguard for Disneyland Paris for about a year and a half—which took me, now a big fish, out of the small pond I was used to. Now I had a vastly wider net of stories to listen to—and they were from tourists and colleagues from different countries, cultures, ages, genders, and walks of life. From lifeguarding to life-coaching, I've seen it all. Ironically, I'm "saving" more lives now than I did poolside.

2) I moved to the UK.

I then moved from France to the UK. Have you ever been totally immersed in a new country and new culture where you barely spoke the language? It's not too different from the experience of a baby learning to... *be human*. By nature, I was the most observant I'd ever been in my entire life. In learning how to adapt to this new culture as an adult, I learned more about human nature and behaviour than I ever had before in my life.

3) I spent eight years as part of the cabin crew for British Airways.

This was the big one that really fed and restructured my identity as a coach, philosopher, and observer. Working for British Airways, I travelled the world. Thanks to this job, I have literally flown with thousands of people (crew and passengers)—and there's no more diverse melting pot. Even though they were strangers, people seemed to open up to me so quickly. I have a theory that this happened because most people don't get the chance to talk about themselves much to someone who genuinely just wants to listen. Sensing my genuine interest and curiosity in their lives, the flood gates opened. I heard it all; their fears, doubts, problems, sex life, money stuff, the struggles, the successes, happiness, victories, hobbies, relationship good and bads, the list never ends. For me, it was a blessing. In the air, I had the patience and the time, plus the tools and awareness from my upbringing to analyse their problems and truly help these people.

4) I taught skiing and snowboarding.

Funny—you teach for the sake of helping *others* learn, but you learn so much yourself as a teacher. I have taught skiing and snowboarding on and off during days off, holidays, and sometimes full-time for the past 14 years. I live in a place called Milton Keynes in the UK, where there is an indoor ski dome called Snozone with "real" snow so people can ski and board all year round. I have taught thousands of people through the years. On a busy day, I'd sometimes teach nearly one hundred people in total. Once again, this job gave me the unique opportunity to connect with a wide variety of strangers on a personal level. And against the backdrop of extreme sports, these people came to me with doubt in their own ability, fear of getting injured, and their fear of looking silly in open view—which meant I was teaching a lot more than just technical instruction of the sports. I was micro-coaching every person I worked with so that their doubts and fears wouldn't ruin their experience.

So what?

The through-line throughout all these experiences could be distilled to one common denominator. No matter the uniform I was wearing, I was actually always doing the same job: studying human behaviour and using my findings to affect positive change in people's lives.

These experiences were followed by numerous courses and achievements in the field of life coaching, plus a successful coaching practice of many years. But I still believe the majority of my learning came from my experience "out in the field"—the "field" being *life*.

I am not claiming to know it all or that I'm the go-to expert in human behavioural patterns and beliefs. But Malcolm Gladwell's 10,000 hour rule states that 10,000 hours of deliberate practice in any field will render you a virtuoso. And in their bestseller, *Peak Performance*, Brad Stulberg and Steve Magness further dictate that the 10,000 hour rule does not hold true without the *deliberate, purposeful* practice. Well, I've clocked well over 10,000 hours of the right kind of practice: talking to strangers, compiling research, noticing trends and patterns, testing my findings and hypotheses over and over and over again. Like anything in life, if we spend thousands of hours doing something, we gain mastery of it—especially compared to those who never even give it a second thought.

This book is mostly evidence, observations, and studies, with a small percentage of opinion peppered in. It's not for the close-minded. With this book, I seek to share challenging ideas to encourage people to view their lives and our society through a different lens. According to a 2015 study by influencer marketing agency, Mediakix, the average person will spend more than five years and four months of their lives on social media.[1] That amount of time has likely only increased in recent years. This behaviour has become ingrained in us by this point, and

---

1   "How Much Time Do We Spend on Social Media?" Mediakix.com, accessed May 20, 2018, http://mediakix.com/2016/12/how-much-time-is-spent-on-social-media-lifetime/#gs.jryzpdk.

ingrained behaviour is the toughest to budge without us feeling defensive or attacked. So if you find yourself feeling attacked, join the club! We're all here with you, because this behaviour is ingrained in *all of us*. What is important is what happens *after* you feel defensive: do you keep reading, let your mind fall open, and use this data constructively? Or do you close up and continue living in denial? If you're honestly motivated to change the parts of your life you're unhappy with, then consider the information presented here and then consider merely *adjusting* your relationship with social media. Take what you think is relevant and helpful, leave the rest. As a coach, my only goal has always been to help and as corny as it might sound, if this book does that for anyone, then I've done my job. Knowledge is power, and I want to empower you.

Still wondering "who the hell is this guy?", I'm right there with you. Hey, we are all here to figure out who we are… right? One thing I know for sure is I'm not the enemy here—just the messenger! Please don't shoot! Nothing I write is intended to make fun of, denigrate, or undermine anyone. I am as guilty as you are when it comes to certain aspects of social media, and I'm only trying to help. We're all in the same boat. And though some issues might not apply to you, rest assured that my research and experience proves they definitely apply to others, and it might be helpful for you to learn about how social media is affecting others in different ways than it affects you.

Most importantly, I invite you to embrace and explore any resistance you might have to reading this book because if there's anything I've learned, it's that resistance indicates a resonant truth… perhaps one that you just don't want to hear. An alcoholic defensively *swears* they don't have a problem because… they actually do have a problem; in the same breath, I have clients defensively *swear* their overabundance of selfies are really "just for them" because… they're actually very much not. Your fondness for your phone and social media is what doesn't want you to read this book. And frankly, my own fondness (I'm human, too!) is what didn't want me to write it. This technology has become an ingrained part of all of us… but the question remains: *at what cost?*

O N E

The Good News First

> "When you give everyone a voice and give
> people power, the system usually ends up in a
> really good place."
>
> – Mark Zuckerberg

Sure, we all know that social media is… awesome. Otherwise, it wouldn't have exploded in popularity as it has today. But just because we know something feels good doesn't necessarily mean we've mindfully assessed why it *is* good. To understand where we've gone *wrong* with social media, we must first understand where we've gone *right*.

So… what's the whole point of social media?

It may seem obvious, but if you actually give it a think, it's clear we've lost touch with the actual demand social media was created to answer. Facebook, Instagram, YouTube, Twitter, and Snapchat are all different social media apps, but were they created for the same fundamental reason?

Do they each answer the same societal question, despite offering different features? Let's take a closer look at the four most popular ones. This ain't Wikipedia, so I won't bore you with too many details.

The one that started it all: Facebook

Sure, MySpace was first, but Facebook made a much bigger splash. It was originally launched on February 4th, 2004, but was limited to Harvard Students (so... *not* me). By September 26th, 2006, it became open to everyone above the age of 13 years old.

I am not that old, but I'm definitely old enough to actually remember when Facebook "arrived." I was working for British Airways at the time. I kept receiving texts and emails saying so-and-so was inviting me to join Facebook. For some reason, I was super reluctant to join. I'm not sure why, but for months I ignored them all. I kept hearing people at work talking incessantly about Facebook and finally I caved in and joined. It wasn't because of peer pressure—I truly felt none. Rather, the idea started to sound more appealing the more I heard about it.

According to my Facebook timeline, I joined in April 2007. Wow, that was 11 years ago! 11 years?! Where has all that time gone? I remember the excitement of creating this new online identity: populating my Facebook with a profile picture (after desperately searching for a decent one), an "about me", my favourite movies, favourite books (okay, there weren't too many books at the time), and searching for friends that I may have known. I also remember that adding random people wasn't such a big deal at all back then. Yes, I was totally guilty of this among other common social media behaviours: adding random strangers for the mere thrill of seeing your friend list get bigger and bigger. If you were one such stranger I haphazardly "friended," please accept my deepest apologies; let's just say that I was young and silly. For you readers that I haven't added yet… um, friend me please? Haha! I'm only *half* kidding. Suffice to say, it didn't take too long for me to be a loyal Facebook convert. Once I fully embraced it, I became the one sending numerous Facebook invitations to friends and family members.

As mentioned above, at the time I was working for British Airways as a cabin crew member. I was flying around Europe, so with family and old friends being in France, it was a great way to share my adventures with them. I really enjoyed creating albums chronicling my different destinations so that they could discover the world along with me in a way. At that time, I never felt the urge to use Facebook the way more and more people use it now: to show off, boost self-esteem, advertise every mundane detail of our lives, or debate ad nauseam. The things I shared were created for the sole purpose of, well, unselfishly *sharing*. And I think that's how everyone used Facebook in its early days.

Now, Facebook is a force to be reckoned with as statistically the most popular social media platform.

According to a recent article published by Wordstream,[2] Facebook has about 2.01 billion monthly active users as of June 30, 2017. Looking at just the United States for example, 79% of Americans use Facebook, and more than half (53%) of U.S. residents use Facebook several times per day. This book will examine stats in plenty of different countries—but don't get too caught up in which nation is which—social media is globally applicable, and the trends throughout every country typically mirror each other proportionately. 400 new users create Facebook accounts every *minute*, and 22% of the world's total population uses Facebook. Each day, 35 million people update their Facebook statuses. But if there's any stat to consider, it's this one because money always talks: last year, Facebook exceeded $500 billion in market value for the first time.[3]

Instagram, who?

Instagram was launched for iPhone in October 2010, and then two years later on Android. Once again, I was reluctant to join at first, especially since I thought Facebook was perfectly sufficient when it came to sharing pictures. BUT of course, I was only human, the idea seduced me eventually,

---

2   Gordon Donnelly, "75 Super-Useful Facebook Statistics for 2018," Wordstream, accessed May 20, 2018, https://www.wordstream.com/blog/ws/2017/11/07/facebook-statistics.

3   Matt Egan, "Facebook and Amazon hit $500 Billion Milestone," Money. CNN.com, accessed May, 23 2018, http://money.cnn.com/2017/07/27/in-vesting/facebook-amazon-500-billion-bezos-zuckerberg/index.html.

and I ended up joining (though it took some time for me to give up my Blackberry phone first). My first post was on May 11th, 2013. A day after my birthday. It was a little controversial (how dare I!) because it was so politically incorrect. It was an ice cube with paper clip arms and legs, doing bicep curls with a match in his right hand, sweets stuck on each side of the match like a dumbbell, looking at a picture of the Titanic sinking after hitting a massive iceberg, with the caption "If you can dream it, you can achieve it".

My following posts were mostly random photos from my trips, cool quotes I stumbled across, or images that made me laugh. But after using Facebook for so long, the novelty of posting wore off really quickly. The "excitement" wasn't as big with Instagram. If anything, it almost felt like I was obligated to post things, like there was some sort of subconscious pressure around it. I most definitely sensed this with others.

As of 2017, the Mediakix research team estimates that Instagram's market value is over $102 billion, 5x as much as Snapchat, and 6x as much as Twitter.[4] According to a myriad of 2018 studies compiled by Wordstream,[5] there are over 800 million Instagrammers, up from the 600 million at the end of 2016. 80% of those Instagrammers are located outside of the U.S. Out of the 800 million, 500

---

4   "Instagram is Worth Over $100 Billion," Mediakix, accessed May 23, 2018, http://mediakix.com/2017/12/how-much-is-instagram-worth-market-cap/#gs.=Ik7B3E.

5   Mary Lister, "33 Mind-Boggling Instagram Stats & Facts for 2018," Wordstream, accessed May 23, 2018, https://www.wordstream.com/blog/ws/2017/04/20/instagram-statistics.

million are active every single day. 35% of users report they look at the platform several times per day. 95 million photos and videos are shared on Instagram per day.

Youtube—TV's social media replacement

Created February 14, 2005, it was as if the founders somehow knew society was embarking on a long love affair with this technological Valentine. However, it took over two months for the first video to be uploaded on April 23rd, 2005, and it was a video made by one of the founders! Perhaps it took some time to gain momentum because there was some mystery around *why* exactly YouTube was created in the first place. It certainly wasn't answering some dire demand. If anything, its creation boiled down to one thing: feeding the belief that your home videos are as interesting—if not more—than what you see on TV.

Great! Thanks guys! Thanks to you founders, I've literally burnt thousands and thousands of hours watching random crap on YouTube! We're all guilty of this, right? Simple example: while writing this chapter, I was simultaneously planning a trip to visit my editor in New York, friends in Montreal, and then my friend in Toronto. I quickly googled trains from New York to Montreal, which by the way is a journey over ten hours long and it isn't a sleeper train! Nonetheless, I was excited about it so I thought I'd look online to see if there were any pics available from the inside of the train. After not much luck with Google images,

I thought to check for YouTube videos and WHAT A MISTAKE I made. I skimmed through two videos (one was over two hours long of landscapes). And then I fell down a rabbit hole of clicking the videos from the "recommended videos" column that captured my interest. Hell, I watched a ten minute long video of a winter snow plough locomotive just doing its job.

It is so easy to get *YouTube* interested in random stuff. I write "Youtube interested" because it's a different brand of interest and curiosity when you're surfing YouTube; everything suddenly seems interesting there. For example, once I watched quite a few videos on how to get rid of hornets nests. One of the videos had more than ten million views, yet I doubt there are millions of people concerned with having to get rid of a hornets nest… I definitely didn't have that problem, but there I watching it anyway! By the time I realised I'd fallen down a YouTube rabbit hole, 45 minutes of wasted time had flown by and I still hadn't decided if I wanted to take the train to Montreal.

According to recent studies,[6] YouTube is the world's second largest search engine—that's right, it's a social media platform and search engine in one. It's also the third most visited site after Google and Facebook. There are over 1.57 billion total monthly active YouTube users,[7]

6   Kit Smith, "39 Fascinating and Incredible YouTube Statistics," Brand-watch.com, accessed May 23, 2018, https://www.brandwatch.com/blog/39-youtube-stats/.

7   Salman Aslam, Salman, "YouTube by the Numbers: Stats, Demographics & Fun Facts," Omnicore, accessed May 23, 2018, https://www.omnicorea-gency.com/youtube-statistics/.

and together we watch over one billion hours of YouTube videos a day, more than Netflix and Facebook video combined. And that's no surprise since 400 hours of video are uploaded to YouTube every *minute*. More than half of YouTube views come from mobile devices, and the average mobile viewing session lasts more than 40 minutes. On average, there are 1,000,000,000 mobile YouTube video views per day.

Snapchat—the new reigning king

Snapchat was originally launched as Picaboo on iOS on July 8th, 2011. Sending a picture to one or more friends at once that would then disappear with no lasting effects on your profile opened new doors to new possibilities.

I did join Snapchat, but it was really short lived. I never really embraced it. I was juggling enough social media accounts as it was. It's not as popular as the other three, but it does still boast over 300 million monthly active users and 187 million daily active users, according to 2018 research by Omnicore.[8] The average Snapchat user spends over 30 minutes per day on Snapchat, and the number of daily Snapchat video views amounts to more than 10 billion… so that's no small feat.

I could mention Twitter, Pinterest, Tumblr and many of the others but to be honest, they are all very similar.

---

8   Salman Aslam, "Snapchat by the Numbers: Stats, Demographics & Fun Facts," Omnicore, accessed May 23, 2018, https://www.omnicoreagency.com/snapchat-statistics/.

The companies don't really matter—it is not about one or the other. There's nothing particularly right about any one company, nor anything particularly wrong with any one. It's simply the concept of them as a whole that has impacted our lives so profoundly. After all, no one at Facebook, Instagram, YouTube, or Snapchat is ordering any of us to spend our lives glued to them, compare ourselves to the people we follow, and feel like crap. And in the same breath, I know there are plenty of people—many of whom I know personally, like my own dad—who do not have any issues with social media. They use it, but somehow avoid letting it subconsciously affect them in a negative way. The difference lies in how we use social media and how we see its purpose.

How social media benefits the individual.

> "We don't have a choice on whether we do
> social media; the question is how well we do it."
> – Erik Qualman

We know why they were created, but what are they actually doing for us? Are they fulfilling the needs they were set out to fill by their founders? Are they providing more benefits than were originally expected? The people who created these platforms only wanted good things and likely still do. It isn't their fault that plenty of *bad* and *ugly* has come along with the *good*. Though this book will discuss why 24/7 accessibility has been detrimental to us, even that has its benefits, too. Here is an incomplete list of all the positives social media—a.k.a. the world at our fingertips—gives to us and helps us do:

- Discovering new places, people, products
- Exchanging new ideas
- Easily finding like-minded people and organisations to advance our own causes
- Sharing our lives with people we love
- Keeping in touch with people geographically distant
- Communication between people/businesses/ community/charities
- Creating awareness on certain topics, issues, and causes
- Capitalise on opportunities you never would have heard of otherwise
- Using it as an online CV to get a job
- Supporting freedom of speech and giving everyone a voice
- Access to infinite information and education
- Making new friends
- Expanding culture, knowledge, and personal growth
- Finding inspiration
- Starting a business
- Expanding a business
- Participating in debates
- Learning countless skills, subjects, languages, and more through videos uploaded by others

- Finding working professionals
- Potentially finding a romantic partner

Just a glance at this list should tell you that social media is designed to *enable*. It has the potential to make our life so much easier, interactive, sociable and more, *but only* when used and interpreted in a certain way. What way is that? Read on. :)

How social media benefits groups of people.

Okay, I may have given that tricky wording on purpose. When I say "groups of people," I mean companies and corporations. But consider this: companies that do well mean employment, employment means happier people than if they were jobless. Social media companies have more in mind than just profits. They all began with vision for a different, better future that would fundamentally change the way we live, communicate, interact, relate with businesses and products, get our news about the world, donate to charities, organise events, and the list goes on and on. Social media has created a new ecosystem in which we all live. It is almost impossible to not use at least one social media platform today. Many people might not have Facebook, Instagram, Snapchat, or Twitter, but they likely visit YouTube regularly. Our society has become too visually-oriented to avoid that.

Look at Kim Kardashian. I am not for or against her. And whether you love her or hate her, there is no denying the fact that she has managed to utilise social media at its maximum. Instagram is a primary moneymaker for her, where she can make over $300,000 per sponsored post.[9] She and her family have made social media their primary way of communicating and doing business, and Kim was the first one to really create an empire sprung from social media. She and her whole business have benefited tremendously from the identity she has created purely through the mobile device.

Keep this all in mind as you continue reading. I did not write this book to demonise social media, but rather to remind us that everything has the *potential* to help us or hurt us—it all depends on how we use it. There's no question that social media is a technological powerhouse. But with great power comes great responsibility... and how responsible are we all really being to ourselves and to each other?

9   Natalie Robehmed, "How Kim Kardashian West Bounced Back To $45.5 Million--And A New Cosmetics Company," Forbes, accessed May 20, 2018, https://www.forbes.com/sites/natalierobehmed/2017/06/13/how-kim-kardashian-west-bounced-back-to-45-5-million-and-a-new-cosmetics-company/.

TWO

And Now the Bad News

If social media was designed to create good things and it has so many benefits, then why are we pointing fingers at it? Why are more and more articles, studies, coverage on TV, and parents fearing for their kids doubting it? Simple. In my interactions with people on both personal and professional levels, I have observed that more and more people are not only negatively affected by social media, but are left with more problems than they started with.

Yeah. Read that again. It is unbelievable to me that no matter their age, gender, job, relationship status, culture, or any other factor, more and more people find their relationship with social media is playing tricks on them. An unhealthy relationship with social media is a common denominator in *almost every person that I help.* And more often than not, they're not even aware of it.

The even crazier part? There are more and more articles and studies out there about our collective relationship with social media, but fewer books. Perhaps this is because we're subconsciously defensive and protective of our relationships with social media. That's understandable. According to the titans of the research industry, our eyes are glued to our phones for over four hours each day in 2018.[10] That amounts to over 11 years of our lives. And five years and four months of that time spent on our phone we spend solely on social media.[11] *Five years and four months.* That's more time than we spend eating and drinking in a lifetime, which is three years and five months. We are addicted to our phones. As is true with any addiction, the more addicted we are to our phones the more we don't *want* them to be the problem. And when I say "we," I'm including myself and people like me—professionals who are trying to change people's lives. It's easy to overlook technology as being the root of our problems... because that's just too easy of an answer, right? Wrong.

The Silent Killer?

It took decades for doctors, researchers, sociologists and the rest of us to fully understand the risks of smoking, drinking, and drugs. Smoking was even encouraged for *decades.* There was a time when it seemed that everyone smoked, and nobody even considered there could be

---

10   Kenneth Burke, "How Much Time Do People Spend on Their Mobile Phones in 2018?" TEXT REQUEST, accessed May 23, 2018, https://www.textrequest.com/blog/how-much-time-people-spend-mobile-phones-2017/.

11   "How Much Time Do We Spend On Social Media," Mediakix, accessed May 23, 2018, http://mediakix.com/2016/12/how-much-time-is-spent-on-social-media-lifetime/#gs.jryzpdk.

negative consequences. Now, the potential fatal effects of smoking are common knowledge. We now have plenty of techniques to help people *stop* smoking or drinking, including support groups and helplines. So in this modern era, when someone decides to smoke, they're well aware of the risks going into it. Obviously, this means people are less inclined to get into it in the first place.

Social media isn't so different. No one joins social media thinking that one day it will cause them problems. Nobody joins thinking that someday, in one way or another, simply being on social media will be a source of struggle. But slowly, the research is catching up with us—just as it did with smoking, for example—to prove to us that social media has a dark side when used in an unhealthy way.

The way that social media *is* different is that its negative effects are much harder to measure than those of smoking or drinking. Now, simple lab tests reveal to us the unfortunate results of mistreating our bodies when abusing substances. But there's no metric to measure unhappiness, no scale to weigh our growing insecurities. And *that's* what makes social media the "silent killer." The negative effects of social media won't ever be revealed to you in lab results from your yearly check-up. Instead, uncovering and facing them requires something much more elusive: honest self-awareness.

What makes it even tougher to "diagnose" is the fact that different generations have different relationships with social media. Our youngest generations have grown up with social media and thereby normalise it—accepting it as a minor detail of daily life that deserves no scrutiny whatsoever. Older generations cannot understand what this is like because they *didn't* grow up with it; in fact, they've lived most of their lives without it.

So, let's say a 17 year old goes to a therapist with a hunch that social media is negatively affecting their life. There's a good chance that the therapist, who may be older, truly cannot relate or understand what this 17 year old is talking about. Likewise, parents are often at a loss, completely missing how social media is negatively affecting their kids simply because they don't understand it themselves. Nonetheless, billions of people use social media, but they themselves also barely understand its repercussions.

I do not claim to be a social media expert, but...

In my line of work, the amount of overlap between unhealthy social media relationships and unhappy people is staggering. Even as I write this chapter, mere minutes ago a friend of mine (not even a client!) just confessed to me how much she has struggled to be popular and liked in the social media world despite not feeling that pressure at all in the real world.

But you don't even have to be a life coach or modern day philosopher like me to recognise that way too many people struggle and often suffer from the whole social media thing. Either they waste precious time and energy agonising over how to "behave" on social media or they let it consistently make them feel like they're not enough. And the reason why this problem is so widespread is because it's *very hard* to pinpoint social media as being the root cause. Of course if you don't know what's causing the issue, you can't change it. If you keep getting stomach aches but you have no clue you're intolerant to a food you regularly eat, you don't know to stop eating it. Often, we make matters worse by trying to correct *other* things that are not the root causes, and thereby create new problems in the process.

The Truth:

If you're human, you're likely misusing social media. That's actually a relief because it means it's nobody's fault; rather, it's just human nature! The sooner you can become aware of your relationship and determine how it's harming you, the sooner you can start using social media in a way where it does nothing but *serve* you.

But how can this be a problem for everyone if we're all *unique?*

You may be thinking, "But how can this life coach help me without knowing *me*?" I may not know you personally, but I've helped (and witnessed in agony) enough people for whom social media is a big enough (and often unrecognised) concern that I thought it best to write a book to help a wider net of people. If you can read this with an open mind and remember that I'm just like you—I've shared your struggles and I'm on your side—then there may be some nuggets of wisdom that you can glean from this book. All my experiences, observations, and the studies and statistics are for *your benefit*. Maybe not everything will apply to you, but chances are there is at the very least something that will.

Maybe you're a kid who's grown up with a phone attached to your hand, developmentally shaping your (lack of) confidence, and your parents have no idea how to help you. Maybe you're a young professional whose self-esteem takes a daily beating because you're addicted to comparing your life to the lives of everyone you follow on social media. Maybe you're someone in a healthy relationship, yet you're letting social media harm or even destroy your relationship. And maybe you feel like you live two lives—the one in which you show your face and the other in which you hide behind your avatar. No matter who you are, no matter what you are, you likely don't even realise how social media is in one way or another likely negatively affecting you or the loop you're stuck in. In fact, you may even believe that you *need* social media in order to feel good because you feed on the attention and validation that social media brings. Or perhaps you simply feel you've been on them for so long that they're a part of who you are, what you do—you write them off as a harmless part of your daily routine!

I was talking about this to a client today. She confessed to doing all she could to increase her followers and likes, including following complete strangers, posting "sexy" pics rather than ones that honestly reflected her identity, and spending time agonising over how to strategically plot her social media popularity. She was doing all of this because she believes it feels nice to be liked, to feel attractive, and to gain confidence. I asked her how long she'd been relying on social media to fill that hole in her life, to which she responded, "A little over a year—ever since my break-up with my ex-boyfriend." I then asked if she *did* get lots of likes that made her feel good every time she posted something. She said yes. I logically concluded that a year of doing that should mean she should surely feel amazing by now, full of confidence, self esteem, etc. She said no; at best she is feeling the same, at worst probably even worse. I wasn't surprised by her answer. So why does she keep doing it? It's easy to become addicted to things that are bad for us without realising they're bad to begin with.

What makes matters worse is that social media is used by everyone… and nobody seems to be aware of the negative effects. Smoking, drinking and working too hard are also things we become addicted to that harm us, but all of those things are much more conditional than social media. Unlike social media, they don't affect everyone at every age, every sex, from every culture, every country, at every stage of life. That's why social media is so much more dangerous than the rest. Engaging in social media is learned behaviour that we practice *everywhere*—

on public transportation, walking down the street, in bed, waiting in line, on the toilet. Nothing stops us from tapping that glowing icon on our phones. Even if you manage to kick the habit, you still are bombarded with constant reminders and notifications to encourage you to get back on the social media bandwagon. In fact, psychologists use the term "social contagion" to define moods and behaviours spreading from person to person—in other words "copycat behaviour." The word "contagion" is related to one we often use to describe the transmission of disease: contagious. In that same way, we're able to transmit emotional states and behaviours as well. Social media illustrates that perfectly.

In defence of… well… all of us, it's easier to become addicted to social media than it is to anything else. The first and most obvious reason is that we access it via our phones, and our phones are likely on us at all times. The second is that more and more of our communication is conducted through social media platforms. For example, I personally speak to many people through Facebook, but I don't have their phone numbers. That is why social media addiction has a much larger impact than, say, video game addiction. If you're not at home, you can't use your video console. And if you don't have a video console, then you definitely can't play a video game (lol).

BUT the problem is not social media in itself.

Like any product, its creators certainly wanted people to get hooked on social media... but that's just the nature of any business venture. That aside, social media doesn't purposefully emit some carefully designed subliminal messaging that forces us to spend hours scrolling through them or posting 100 selfies per day. The issue lies in how, when, where, and why people use social media. As we saw in the last chapter, social media has its benefits, and it definitely deserves a place in our evolving society. But we are relying on social media to fulfil needs it was never designed to fulfil. That bears repeating: we depend on social media to fulfil needs it was never designed to fulfil—so not only do those needs *not* get met, we end up feeling worse from our constant futile attempts to squeeze blood from the social media stone.

The social media problem is similar to the microwave problem. Microwaves on their own aren't bad. But the introduction of the microwave lead to a spike in microwave meals, which thereby encouraged bad eating habits and a host of following problems, including obesity.[12] Microwaves don't necessarily *cause* obesity. Rather, it's how we use microwaves that has led to it.

And if neither of those examples speak to you, try thinking of it this way: if phones didn't have cameras,

---

12   Roger Highfield, "Microwave Sparked Obesity Epidemic," The Telegraph, accessed May 23, 2018, https://www.telegraph.co.uk/news/uknews/1553734/Microwave-sparked-obesity-epidemic.html.

would you buy throwaway cameras, take dozens of pictures of yourself, and distribute them to friends and strangers alike? How would doing that make you feel?

We turn to social media for the wrong reasons, use it in a way it wasn't necessarily intended to be used, and then end up really struggling to feel good about ourselves, our homes, our communities, our lives. We develop anxiety, depression, guilt, and jealousy without ever really understanding why. To change the way we use social media, we need to understand first exactly how we're misusing it and how it makes us feel like crap more effortlessly than anything else can.

The end goal is to change our strategies, perspectives, and beliefs about social media. This will allow for gradual change or even overnight change (I've witnessed it!) so that you can actually start *being* the person you want to be— not the one merely putting on a show for your followers. We all have the potential to get there one way or another. Like learning any new skill, it just takes practice. Turns out practice is just as necessary for *unlearning*—as is the case with social media.

I remember teaching snowboarding once to a guy who was extremely overweight. He couldn't buckle his own straps on the board. I helped him but I could see he was really mad at himself. I saw him again around six months later, and he was slimmer! I asked him, "What happened?!" He replied that when he couldn't do his own straps by himself in that first lesson with me, the shame he felt was the nail in the coffin that made him decide enough was enough—he was going to lose the weight. And he did! Fast. On the other hand, a friend of mine took nearly two years to lose the weight he wanted. But he ultimately did it. In the end, they both got to who they wanted to be and how they wanted to feel. It isn't a race, it is a marathon!

Disclaimer

If you recognise elements of yourself as you read onwards, please don't take offence. Rather, rejoice at the possibility that this simple awareness and consequent alterations to your lifestyle could affect your life positively in *massive* ways. I think you're *incredible* for being open-minded enough to put yourself under your own microscope and for being committed to self-improvement (which we ALL should be!). Hey, I'm not pretending to be Freud here. This isn't a name-and-shame nor an encyclopedia documenting people's social media no-nos. When I tell you about a client I worked with or a friend I observed, it isn't to make fun of that person. Rather, those references serve as anecdotal evidence of very serious issues I want to bring to your attention. It's not some strange brand of voyeurism or self-serving nosiness for me. In fact, this is not about me in any way whatsoever. This is just an effort to make your lives better and the evolution of our society more positive.

Remember that using social media is a learned behaviour. It's not like breathing, which we've done since birth. Social media was introduced to us, we learned to use it a certain way, and we are completely able to relearn how to use it in a different way to better serve us. The many ways we do use it—including the potentially harmful ways—have been normalised, which means you might not see exactly how they can be negative at first. But just because a behaviour has been normalised doesn't mean it's right.

I'm not here to dictate what to post and what not to post or threaten your freedom of speech (or freedom of Instagramming!). I'm simply here to empower you to make sure you really *are* freely posting what serves you, your own greater good, and the good of others. You don't need people to like your selfies in order to be happy. You don't need to share your relationship with nameless followers in order to be happy. In fact, pursuing those things could ultimately be contributing to that stagnant *unhappiness* you can't seem to shake.

If you find yourself feeling defensive, maybe rationalising for example, "No, I post loads of selfies because I am a model and I'm promoting my business," I only ask that you take a breath, open yourself up to the possibility that there's something you *could* adjust here, and keep reading. Most people who post loads of selfies, exaggerate their lifestyles, and use social media to make up for lacking confidence are typically not aware of any of this, or a part of them is but they're stuck in total denial. These upcoming shocking statistics don't lie, and we're all part of those statistics *together*—me included. We're all in the same boat and I am certainly not the captain of it. And the only person you could be butting heads with is *yourself*. With social media, if there's any opposition, it's always you vs. you because it's only about *your* life, *your* choices, *your* future. The studies, statistics, and facts are out there. It's up to you if you want to face them. And I'll be honest: I don't have the solution. But I do know that awareness is the first step to *any* solution, and that's what we're doing together with this book.

Granted, there *are* people out there who do not have issues with social media and many who are not even on social media! It's important to remember that those people not only exist, but they're successful people advancing their careers, they thrive easily with purpose in our modern society, and they are wildly happy in their personal and social lives.

So. Could you give up your social media for a week? A month? A year? Forever? If even one of those options makes you nervous, then you deserve to ask yourself "Why?" You are worth exploring that answer. And if at any point you feel attacked or mocked or targeted, then flip back to this disclaimer and remember that I've *always* got your back.

"You can't change what you refuse to confront."

– John Spence

THREE

No Kidding (Or Adulting)— The Danger Starts Young

"It is easier to build strong children than to repair broken adults."

— F. Douglass

I can imagine that it can be very tricky for parents to deal with their kids using social media. In fact, I *know* it to be tricky for them. Social media opens the door to many things that parents have no control over: the images they're seeing, the strangers they're communicating with, the information about themselves they're sharing, and far more. And if the parents are not too into social media themselves, it's even harder for them to understand how it all works, how great an impact it can have, and how to monitor it.

Most people don't realise that we treat our kids the way the paparazzi treat movie stars. We are constantly asking them to smile or to pose and snapping photos of them. In the world of "sharenting," more than 80% of children are said to have an online presence by the age of two and the average parent shares nearly 1,500 images of their child online before they turn five.[13] In one New York Times article, a parent describes what it's like having a three-year old who says "take a picture" before he and his wife even grab their phones and who loves scrolling through photos of herself to pass the time.[14] The problem here is that we are breeding our kids to be picture-obsessed. The online presence of kids makes it even easier for parents to also project their own agendas onto their kids; for example, getting them into modeling. We are teaching young kids some really bad habits, beliefs, and a brand of self consciousness at the only time in life when they can truly afford to lose themselves in their lack of self-awareness and simply just *be*.

If you don't have kids, you might think that this isn't a chapter for you. But do you have younger siblings, nephews or nieces, and cousins? Do you babysit? Do you plan to become a parent some day? It might be smart to start thinking about this now and save yourself the time and headaches down the road. And even if you have zero

---

13 Claire Bessant, "Do parents share too many pictures of their child online?" International Business Times, accessed May 24, 2018, https://www.ibtimes.co.uk/do-parents-share-too-many-pictures-their-children-online-1640174.

14 David Zweig, "Why We Should Take Fewer Pictures of Our Children," The New York Times, accessed May 24, 2018 https://parenting.blogs.nytimes.com/2012/10/12/why-we-should-take-fewer-pictures-of-our-children/.

kids in your life and *never* plan to, the truth is that you were a child once too. Even if you were already an adult when social media was born, chances are you reacted as all of us did: like a kid with a new toy. Frankly, everything in this chapter that applies to kids applies to adults too. The risks of social media are pretty much the same for all of us, no matter our age. I say "pretty much" because I think most youngsters can be much more prone to peer pressure than adults who just don't give a shit anymore! The other difference is that kids are at a key point when social and communication skill development is more fragile and active, so effects might be stronger for someone starting to use social media at age 10 versus someone starting at age 40. "Prevention is better than cure," so it's beneficial to correct unhealthy behaviours and beliefs before they're set in stone and are much harder to adjust later on in life.

Now this is definitely not a chapter about good or bad parenting. I am no child psychologist nor am I in any position to preach to you about how to raise your kids. However, when it comes to social media, I do have plenty of information to supply you with so that you can go on to make your own informed decisions. An American Academy of Pediatrics News magazine article published in January 2015 reported, "a recent study found that nearly 60 percent of children use social media by age 10."[15] In fact, studies show that teenagers between the ages of

---

15 Rebecca Granet, "Living In Live Time: Social Media's Impact On Girls," CBS New York, accessed May 24, 2018, http://newyork.cbslocal. com/2016/09/19/social-media-use-teens/.

12–17 use text messaging more than any other form of communication, including face-to-face interaction.[16] Knowing this, it's a no-brainer that social media is having *some* effect on kids and their development. I just want to raise awareness of potential behaviours, beliefs, and side effects that you might have noticed with your kids and youngsters in your life—because perhaps you haven't made the connection between those effects and social media. And with social media so ubiquitous in their lives, it's tough to pinpoint those connections!

This awareness is powerful because how we interact socially is a *learned behaviour*. So that means we can unlearn a social behaviour as quickly as we first learned it! We simply need to be aware of the negative effects to begin with in order to change it. As a parent, being there for the kids in your life can help cultivate this awareness in them. This is the single most important thing we can do for them regarding their relationship with social media, otherwise we are borderline micromanaging them in an unhealthy way that could cause more problems in the long run. After all, we can't magically make them *not* feel low self esteem, for example, in response to what they see on Instagram. But we *can* help, discuss, and support them in how they process the experience and their feelings.

As you know, a lot of this also comes from the example we set. Sure, we can't force them to feel or not feel a certain

---

16   A. Lenhart, K. Purcell, A. Smith, K. Zickur, "Social Media and Young Adults," Washington, DC: Pew Research Center; 2010, accessed May 24, 2018, http://pewinternet.org/Reports/2010/Social-Media-and-Young-Adults.aspx.

way, but we can set an example to help support healthy behaviour and belief systems. Speaking of examples, here is the perfect one to demonstrate how setting an example would apply to social media. A friend of mine was really worried because her young daughters were posting loads of selfies on social media, already trying to look "sexy". I asked her if her daughters followed her on social media and she said that they did. I then asked what about how she behaves on her social media accounts? Full disclosure: I already knew the answer to this because we follow each other. She told me that she had loads of sexy pics, selfies, and so on. I'm not saying that if you set a great example, your kids will be exemplary, but most "bad" stuff is picked up at school, with friends, and at home. So do your bit at the very least—control what you *can* control! Kids are smart and if they are exposed to the "bad" at school, they'll notice the difference between that and the "good" at home, and exercise decision-making that's crucial to their development as full human beings.

It's never too late.

If you do have kids, you might be thinking, "This is great, but my kids are already young adults and they have been using social media for years now." As a coach, I can tell you that nothing is <u>ever</u> too late. Even the slightest of changes in people can create totally different behaviour— no matter their age. I know this because I coach people of all ages, and I've seen it!

"Different generation, different technology!"

I vividly remember my parents rambling on about how when they were younger, they didn't have TVs, video games, or mobile phones. They boasted about how they would be out playing or reading books. I would think to myself, "That's great, guys. Thanks for the lecture, but it isn't your time anymore and things have changed." Funny as I've gotten older, I've caught myself rambling on to younger generations the same way my parents once did. But some mental gymnastics is required for working around the part of that which is just our natural resistance to change and our loyalty to the way things were when we grew up, versus the changes that actually are unbiasedly harmful. If we said to every older person reminiscing about the past "You just don't understand—times have changed," then that would imply that our culture has changed *only* in a beneficial way as time has gone on, and that's simply not true. Just as there are constant new positives, there are always new negatives too.

Facebook was available for the general public in 2006, Instagram in 2010 (iOS) and 2012 (Android), Snapchat in 2011, and Twitter in 2006. All in all, quite recent. But just as our parents may have limited television when it was a novelty, you have every right to limit phone time, too. Maybe social media isn't allowed in the evenings. Maybe the rule is that you follow your kids so that you can monitor their activity. No matter what rules you're comfortable with, *simply having rules* is good. Why? Because it communicates that social media shouldn't be the axis upon which your kid's life spins. Rather, it should be what maybe TV was to you: a treat. A part of life that enriches it. Not a tyrant who rules it.

The challenges...

1) Bullying, cyberbullying, and harassment.

These three go hand-in-hand, and they definitely affect kids more than adults. Online, it's too easy for kids to participate in harassment of any kind. Most kids who do bully and harass don't even realise that they do it and even worse, they do it to feel better about themselves. And do you think social media is helping this problem or making it worse? One of the primary risks of social media is that it makes people feel bad about themselves, so pair that with a kid who is already bullying and you've got a recipe for disaster. According to an article by New York Behavioral Health, "Cyberbullying refers to using digital media to communicate false, embarrassing or hostile information about another person and it is the most common risk for all teens. Cyberbullying can happen to anyone and often causes psychological problems such as depression, anxiety, isolation and even suicide."[17]

---

17 "The Impact of Social Media Use on Social Skills," accessed May 24, 2018, http://newyorkbehavioralhealth.com/the-impact-of-social-media-use-on-social-skills.

Phones plus the anonymity that social media facilitates has also made cyberbullying easier than ever before. "According to British anti-bullying organization Ditch The Label's annual survey, Instagram was the most widely used cyberbullying network in 2017, with 42 percent of those cyberbullied reporting that Instagram was the network of choice."[18] Statistically speaking, more people are bullying and being bullied than ever before because it's easy to hide behind a keyboard. "Traditional" bullying could happen only face to face. Social media allows it to happen anytime, anywhere, as frequently as the bully would like. The biggest issue with bullying and harassment is that most kids won't confess it is happening to them. This is where open communication and paying close attention to your kid's behaviour will increase your chances of finding out if your kid is being bullied.

2) Child grooming.

Grooming is when someone (often a stranger online) builds an emotional connection with a child to gain their trust for the purposes of sexual abuse, sexual exploitation, or trafficking. Unfortunately, it has never been easier to get away with than it is today. Grooming has increased at an alarming rate due to the role phones and social media play in our lives because they make it much easier to access

---

18 Mary Lister, "33 Mind-Boggling Instagram Stats & Facts for 2018," accessed May 23, 2018, https://www.wordstream.com/blog/ws/2017/04/20/instagram-statistics.

children. In 2016–2017, over 2,100 counselling sessions with young people who talked to Childline about online child sexual exploitation took place and the Internet Watch Foundation identified over 57,000 URLs in 2016 containing child sexual abuse images.[19]

Again, social media definitely offers some amazingly positive opportunities. It also has a very dark side and grooming is part of that. I am NOT saying that social media promotes, creates, or encourages it. I am saying that people use social media as a vehicle to facilitate their wrong-doings. It is much easier to create a fake account and try to converse online than it is to wait outside a school and chat up a kid there.

I remember watching a program a few years ago about an undercover police officer catching a guy who was chatting with a 14 year old girl, first as "friends", then later down the line started to talk about meeting up in a park to "hug". Luckily on that occasion, the girl ended up telling her parents and therefore, the police could be alerted. You can easily imagine how totally different and potentially atrocious things could have ended up being.

Disgustingly, the number of such cases is escalating at a terrifying rate and that is only including the cases that are being reported. Imagine if all the ones that have been kept secret were also included in that number. As we will see later on, one of the major potential problems of social

---

19 "Online Abuse Facts & Statistics," accessed May 24, 2018, https://www. nspcc.org.uk/preventing-abuse/child-abuse-and-neglect/online-abuse/ facts-statistics/.

media is the ease of creating fake profiles and personalities. In no time, someone with a twisted mind can create a profile with fake pictures and access millions of kids from their own sofa. I think social media companies should create a way to screen people when they try to open an account, like submitting proof of identity. Social media is marketed as a place to communicate with your *friends*. In a kid's mind, there's nothing wrong with chatting with a new "friend," which makes it even harder for parents to detect. Considering the current trend, this will only get worse unless we make a change.

3) False perceptions of the world at large.

This is a symptom we see in countless people, regardless of their age or stage in life, and we'll delve into it more deeply in Chapter 6. It is a big problem for everyone as let's face it, most people on social media carefully curate what they show and what they keep secret. We have full control over portraying the identity we *want* to portray—not necessarily who we really are. There is no malice in this, but it does create a false sense of reality that makes others assume our lives are perfect. Also, you're more likely to get followers by targeting a certain audience. This also affects how we curate our content and is further evidence that it's not a complete, honest reflection of ourselves. In actuality, social media is closer to an art form than it is to an identification form. Yet, we all take it at face value.

Despite this issue being problematic for everyone, it is definitely more applicable to kids simply because where they are in their lives: learning about new things, creating their personal values, discovering who they are, and consciously crafting *who they want to be* as adults. So of course, you can easily imagine how social media's effect on this could be good or not so good. If a kid grows up around gangs, their chances of being in a gang themselves are much higher. If a kid is exposed extensively to something on social media, it's likely to increase their chances of being involved in that something in their own lives.

4) It's hard to create an identity while being pulled in every direction.

Kids are sponges; they absorb everything around them, good and bad. Fast forward a few years and that sponge is now a young adult with values, rules, a personality, and ideas of their own. A concept that is natural, I've been there, so have you and so has everyone else. BUT that natural process of simply growing up, maturing, becoming oneself can become quite tricky when pulled in countless directions. Before social media, you would have a rather finite amount of influence because kids are sheltered to a certain extent: that influence boils down to family, a group of friends, with perhaps minimal exposure to entertainment. These people would be your role models, inspirations, and paradigms. But social media has widened that small circle of influence to be somewhat endless. Now it's flipped: we have constant access to the influence of entertainment, Hollywood celebrities and YouTube celebrities alike, and Instagram strangers galore right in the palm of our hands. It's impossible to have that 24/7 access to even our own families and friends.

Social media is an ever-evolving, infinite stream of influence. Kids already struggle to fit in at school and keep up with the trends of their friends. What happens when it's social media that they're looking up to? An endless struggle that's impossible to "win". How do you discover and create your identity when you're more concerned with keeping up with what's cool? Honestly, people have struggled with this enough *without* social media.

On top of that, there's peer pressure. Yes, peer pressure isn't new at all. But the age of *instant gratification* gives us much less time to think and mull over decisions, making peer pressure more effective. Before social media, you would have had to wait until the next day or the weekend to return to school and face that peer pressure. Now, you get a text, a photo, a video in an instant—and if you wait too long to reply, you might be accused of "ghosting". Speaking of peer pressure...

5) Social media enables peer pressure.

I remember when I was about 15, I lived with my dad in Northern France. A lot of the guys I knew would meet up on the weekends and drink. They always asked me to meet them and do the same, but apart from the fact that it didn't interest me at all, I was super busy pursuing my studies, so even if I wanted to drink, I simply wouldn't have had the time. Funnily enough, for the record, I am now 36 years old and I've never drunk alcohol in my life apart from a sip of wine, champagne, and beer; I've never gotten drunk. Anyway, the point of the story is that there is a massive pressure to do things, be part of things, do what everyone else does because we want to be cool or even just accepted. Sure, that pressure has always existed, but social media has brought that pressure a mere swipe away. That pressure is in our faces all the time. It's no fun at a young age to be rejected, left out, or laughed at! In fact, all that can be incredibly damaging at a young age.

I recently had a conversation with my friend's son and he was telling me that at his school, a lot of the kids would send nude pictures to each other and that his friends questioned why he hadn't sent any. Nude pictures—unless by mail—were never an option prior to phones and social media. Multiply that by the number of friends and the number of years spent at school, and you end up with a shit load of pressure to do plenty of things you don't want to do. It's tough enough handling peer pressure without social media. Add social media to the mix, and navigating peer pressure is closer to navigating a war zone.

6) Communication skills are compromised.

Adolescence is when we begin to forge our characters and develop a wider sense of what's what, the whys, the hows, and new friends we consciously choose rather the ones we simply "fall in with" at school. One of the great things about social media is the ability to connect with literally billions of people from pretty much anywhere around the world. That's amazing. If a kid is learning to speak Spanish, he can easily chat with someone from Spain and improve his skill set. Unfortunately, the flip side is that talking to someone behind a keyboard and a screen is very different to conversing face to face. We heighten our emotional intelligence by interacting with people in real life, reading their facial cues and body language. If we spend our developmental years learning to communicate behind a computer screen, we miss out on essential parts in the development of our communication skills.

My parents continually pushed me out of my comfort zone as a kid. I played different sports, joined new teams, attended new schools, and met new people on a regular basis. This helped me develop the communication skills I needed for my professional life as an adult. The same way that bullies are more likely to bully behind a screen, people are braver when emotionally vulnerable in the digital world as well... but at what cost to their bravery in the real world?

7) Social media addiction is as harmful as any other addiction.

Social media is addictive, plain and simple. In fact, studies estimate that over 210 million people worldwide suffer from internet and social media addictions.[20] It's easier for kids to get addicted than adults because kids have less responsibilities in their lives and therefore, much more time. One of the most miraculous aspects of social media is how it brings the world at our fingertips. We can access anything from anywhere. The ironic part of it is that it's simultaneously the potential biggest problem of social media. Being able to access anything at anytime makes us become dependent on social media so much so that it becomes addictive. Curious about the potential negative consequences of being glued to your phone? There's a whole lot more to come on that.

8) Productivity and creativity suffers.

The reality is that no one can make any real headway on a project while simultaneously glued to their phones, chatting to people, watching random videos, or scrolling through Instagram. We all try to convince ourselves we can, but has that ever actually worked? It simply doesn't

---

20   "These 8 Social Media Addiction Statistics Show Where We're Spending Our Time," Mediakix, accessed May 29, 2018, http://mediakix. com/2018/04/social-media-addiction-statistics/#gs.0MLRSSk.

compute time-wise. Tell a kid to finish their homework while their phone is in front of them. It won't happen. Or it will, but it'll take more time than it would have without the phone.

An obvious contributor to lack of productivity is simply having access to your phone overnight, opening the door to plenty of social media wormholes to fall down and to therefore lose plenty of sleep.

A word on sleep: No, I am not just playing the "when I was younger, we did it *this* way" card, but I will say that traditionally kids have always had earlier bedtimes. When I was growing up, we were not allowed TV during weekdays, we'd be in bed by 9pm, lights out at 9.30pm. We were kids so we were treated like kids. Whether at age 8 or age 14, there was never any *need* to watch TV on a school night and guess what… we all survived.

According to a study by Mediakix,[21] 71% of people sleep with or right next to their mobile phones. Social media isn't just affecting our behaviour during the day—it negatively affects our nights too by damaging our ability to sleep. Roughly 47 million Americans do not get enough sleep and 55% more teenagers were sleep deprived in 2015 than in 1991. Why? Because exposure to screens is largely to thank for worsening sleep disorders. It's been reported that 45% of people check social media *instead* of sleeping. Kids and teenagers are known to require more sleep than

---

21   "These 8 Social Media Addiction Statistics Show Where We're Spending Our Time," Mediakix, accessed May 29, 2018, http://mediakix.com/2018/04/social-media-addiction-statistics/#gs.0MLRSSk.

adults because their brains are still developing… yet 10% of teens check their phones more than 10 times per night. This checks out with what I've observed too; I have heard plenty of the younger generations tell me that they'll be on their phones, chatting with their friends until the early hours of the morning. And why wouldn't they? They're subject to peer pressure, hungry for validation, and they're addicted.

9) Oh, the irony: social media can create an antisocial person.

OK, maybe they're playing games or texting too, but there's no doubt social media consumes a *lot* of phone time. And it's kids and adults alike. How many times have you seen someone on their phone in a group of people, yet they're completely in their own world? Two people on a date where neither person is engaging with each other because they're each glued to their respective phones? Or a gaggle of women at brunch and not one of them is talking because they're *all* on their phones?!

Kasperksy Lab conducted a 2016 study revealing that social media users are interacting less face-to-face than in the past because social media simply offers the *option* of staying in touch online and communicating constantly… not that they necessarily do so. Researchers found that about one third of people communicate less with their parents (31%), partners (23%), children (33%) and friends

(35%) because they can follow them on social media instead.[22]

Social media might make you feel connected to people, but it's no substitute for true social connection. The connection it does facilitate is great in its own right, but don't confuse it for the social life you live in the flesh. Becoming a hermit when you're older is one thing, but becoming one as a teenager deprives you of a better chance of a social future.

10) A recipe for laziness?

One of the last things a parent wants is a lazy kid! As mentioned, I taught skiing and snowboarding on and off for nearly 14 years in an indoor ski dome in the UK. Throughout those years I taught thousands of kids and I can't even tell you how many of them had no hobbies; they weren't interested in sports or music, and they certainly didn't want to be in that indoor ski dome with me. They spent the majority of their time at home playing video games, watching TV, and interacting on numerous social media platforms. It's no surprise they found learning to ski or snowboard a little bit trickier, and oftentimes they'd be so discouraged and uncomfortable out of their comfort zone that they'd never come back for another lesson. Grow that quality into adulthood, and you'll have a person

---

22   "Have we created unsocial media?" Kaspersky Lab Daily, accessed May 24, 2018, https://usa.kaspersky.com/blog/digital-depression/10643/.

who struggles with every curveball life throws at them. Learning and failing is normal and healthy. It's something everyone should experience. Yet, our addiction to social media and screens keeps many of us from ever learning that lesson and becoming comfortable with it.

11) Social media can deprive children of their childhood!

When my younger sister was 15, she wanted to wear high heels because a few girls at her school wore them. I remember my stepmother having a strong reaction. She said, "No way, you're 15! You don't need heels. They're bad for your back especially while you're growing! There is a time and a place for everything—you will have your entire life to wear heels if you want, but 15 isn't the time." That's *high heels*. What about violence, murder, or hardcore porn? All are a click away on a mobile phone. In my line of work, I can't tell you how many parents I've come across who have kids with an unhealthy misconception of what sex is due to what they've seen in porn. According to an article in Psychology Today,[23] research shows that early exposure to pornography increases risk for sex addictions and other intimacy disorders later on in life. Some studies show that exposure to pornography by age 14 may increase the risk

---

23   Carolyn Ross, "Overexposed and Under-Prepared: The Effects of Early Exposure to Sexual Content," Psychology Today, accessed May 24, 2018, https://www.psychologytoday.com/us/blog/real-healing/201208/overexposed-and-under-prepared-the-effects-early-exposure-sexual-content.

of a child becoming a victim of sexual violence or acting out sexually against another child.

These dangers apply to the kid in all of us.

Whether you have kids or not, the truth is that we're all vulnerable to these dangers. Get ready to explore all of them in far more detail and in the context of your adult lives...

FOUR

Social Media's Price Tag: A Bill of *Mental* Health

"Spending just one day away from social media
can be one of the best things you do for your
mental health."

– Unknown

Full disclosure: I am no psychologist or doctor. My goal here is not to delve deep into the science behind this, but rather only to provide you with some basic facts to raise your awareness and put these risks on your radar. Issues like these rarely get better by themselves so if you feel like any of these points speak to you, do not hesitate to seek advice and help from a professional.

We've talked a bit about the very dark side of social media. That's where these potential problems live, too. When misused, social media can enable the tendencies we already have within us to lead an unbalanced life mentally. Once you're in deep, it can be tricky to change things. It's not impossible—it's just harder to work backwards than to avoid it in the first place. Here again, an ounce of prevention is worth a pound of cure. But you can't prevent something of which you have zero awareness.

Many people do not link their lack of self esteem with what they see or read online. In fact, sometimes when I suggest the connection, they defend that behaviour so viciously, it only verifies to me that it is a *huge* contributing factor. It's even harder to make anyone consider social media could be the problem because it's still a new frontier—psychologists and researchers are still trying to map out the full extent of the effects of social media in our everyday life. Nonetheless, more and more research is showing that the connection is quite strong, and studies show that 60% of social media users report social media affecting their self esteem in a negative way.[24] And even if people do have access to studies to connect their issues with social media, getting them to *act* on it is a whole different challenge. Knowledge is power, but you only exert that power if you use the knowledge to take action. As the saying goes, "you can lead a horse to water, but you can't make it drink." Too many people want change and yet they are not willing to change themselves in order to get it.

The truth is that everything this book addresses is rooted in mental health. However, we still treat mental health issues quite primitively because they're not as easy to measure and diagnose as, say, a broken leg. We'll be

---

24   Clarissa Silva, "Social Media's Impact on Self Esteem," HuffPost, accessed May 24, 2018, https://www.huffingtonpost.com/entry/social-medias-impact-on-self-esteem_us_58ade038e4b0d818c4f0a4e4.

exploring in much greater depth how social media impacts our minds and mental states, but here's a brief overview.

Low self-esteem versus low self-confidence.

A lot of people get self-esteem and self-confidence mixed up; social media can compromise both. They sound very similar for sure but they are actually totally different. Yes, they can be complementary and having one can encourage having the other, but fundamentally they are different. Confidence means assurance of your own abilities. Self-esteem is the value you hold for yourself as a human being or your certainty of your own worth. For example, I could be very confident when it comes to how I do my job, but that does not imply that I think highly of myself, respect myself, or feel worthy. Or on the other hand, I could have a great opinion of myself while having low confidence in doing something specific, like speaking to people.

Confidence is tricky because even if you think you don't have it, you likely do. In fact, I've never met someone who doesn't have it. I've had hundreds of clients say to me, "I'm not a confident person." I always ask them, "Is there anything you're pretty good at?" They always give me a list. Always. Nobody has ever said, "No, there's nothing." If you're able to list even *one* thing that you're good at, then you're displaying confidence. For example, if a client were to say that they're confident when playing football, I'd ask that client, "Were you always confident playing football?"

The answer is always, "No, I had to learn and practice and improve." This is evidence that confidence is about perspective. If you attempt something *knowing* it requires the natural process of practice, then you're likely to gain confidence. If you attempt that same thing and expect to get it right that first time, you're disappointed and assume you just "can't do it," leading to lack of confidence. Most of us simply forget the simple principle that **confidence is earned.** If your perspective on confidence is flawed to begin with, then you'll only continue to reinforce that lack of confidence every time you attempt to do something.

As a coach, one of my main strengths is working with people who lack one or both. Both rely on the internal dialogue we are constantly having with ourselves. This dialogue can change—I used to believe certain things about myself that are totally different today. The key is being conscious of this dialogue and saying only to ourselves what we'd say to a loved one.

So how do self-esteem and self-confidence get caught in the crossfire of social media? Because social media directly affects that dialogue you have with yourself. You might think you're interacting with others mostly on social media, but the truth is that when you're scrolling through Instagram or falling down a rabbit hole of random videos, the only conversation you're having is one with yourself in your own head. And if you're bombarded with images and videos of everyone else's "perfect" lives, you're playing the comparison game and how do you think that affects your internal dialogue? Not positively, that's for sure.

Depression and anxiety.

Low self esteem and self confidence are surely gateway issues to diagnosable depression and anxiety. Recent research suggests an undeniable link between social media usage and depression.[25] Research funded by the U.S. National Institutes of Health and published in the journal *Depression and Anxiety* reveals that people who used social media the most were roughly 2.7 times more likely to be depressed than those who used such social media platforms the least. Further research reveals that managing several social media platforms is linked to an even higher risk of depression and anxiety than just using one or two. Researchers assessed how often 1,787 millennials in 2014 checked 11 popular social media networks as well as to what degree they struggle with depression and/or anxiety. Their findings showed that those who used seven or more platforms had more than triple the risk for anxiety and depressive symptoms, compared to those using between zero and two.[26] An even more recent 2018 study found that teenagers who spend five hours per day using their phones were nearly twice as likely to show symptoms of depression than teens who spent only one hour on their phones.[27]

25 Alan Mozes, "The Complex Link Between Social Media and Depression," Health.com, accessed May 21, 2018, http://www.health.com/depression/could-lots-of-time-spent-on-social-media-be-tied-to-depression.

26 Amanda Macmillan, "Millennials Who Use More Social Media Sites Have Higher Depression, Anxiety," Health.com, accessed May 21, 2018, http://www.health.com/depression/multiple-social-media-sites-depression-anxiety.

27 "These 8 Social Media Addiction Statistics Show Where We're Spending Our Time," Mediakix, accessed May 22, 2018, http://mediakix.com/2018/04/social-media-addiction-statistics/#gs.nVGzfck.

If you think higher rates of depression and anxiety don't lead to even worse outcomes, think again. Suicide rates for teens rose between 2010 and 2015, after they had been decreasing for the previous two decades. Examining CDC suicide reports from 2009 to 2015 and results of two surveys given to half a million teens ages 13 to 18, researchers found that teenagers are increasingly depressed, hopeless, and more likely to consider suicide due to an increase in suicide risk factors. Suicide rates jumped in 2012, about the time when smartphones became popular, says researcher Jean Twenge.[28] According to Twenge's study, teens who spend five or more hours per day on their mobile phones are 71 percent more likely to have one risk factor for suicide—regardless of the content being consumed. Considering that studies also show that people spend over four hours on their phones on average, that statistic is pretty scary. In 2015, 36 percent of all teens reported thinking about, planning, or attempting suicide—a substantial increase from 32 percent in 2009. The rates were even higher for girls; from 40 percent in 2009 to 45 percent in 2015.[29]

28   Lulu Garcia-Navarro, "The Risk Of Teen Depression And Suicide Is Linked To Smartphone Use, Study Says," NPR, accessed May 23, 2018, https://www.npr.org/2017/12/17/571443683/the-call-in-teens-and-de-pression.

29   "Rise in Teen Suicide Connected to Social Media Popularity: Study," NYPost.com, accessed May 24, 2018, https://nypost.com/2017/11/14/rise-in-teen-suicide-connected-to-social-media-popularity-study/.

Maybe you do struggle with addiction...

Chances are: you do. Alcohol, drugs, gambling, sugar; maybe you're familiar with one or more, maybe you're not. Maybe you've proudly believed you don't have an addictive personality. But spoiler alert: if you own a device, you likely have an addiction to it to *some* degree. The majority of people I meet do. Social media has been created to be addictive and some researchers even compare its effects to those of cocaine. Dr. Tara Emrani, a psychologist at NYU Langone Health said, "Facebook likes and comments activate similar parts of the brain as opioids, where each like or positive comment activates the reward system and the brain releases dopamine."[30] The fact that most people access social media through their phones[31] and that most people have their phones on them all the time, you can imagine that it is just way too easy to access the social media for no other reason than being unable to sit still with nothing to do for even 30 seconds. Simple example: what do most people do while waiting in line at the post office or bank? Most people, myself included, will be on their phones and what is a resource there with constant new content to entertain us? Social media. That is why most people end up spending on average roughly 1 hour

---

30   Mike Adams, *Is Social Media As Addictive As Cocaine?* High Times, accessed June 11, 2018, https://hightimes.com/news/social-media-addictive-cocaine/.

31   Jay Shemenski. "The Future of Social Media is Mobile. Are You Ready?" Simplymeasured.com, accessed May 23, 2018, https://simplymeasured.com/blog/the-future-of-social-media-is-mobile-are-you-ready/.

and 56 minutes on social media each day.[32] So of course, if most of the distraction available to me comes from social media, chances are I'll become quite dependent on it. And where is the line between dependence and addiction? Is there one or are those two things the same? When does it become unhealthy? Try being without your phone for one day. If it feels challenging, then I'd venture to say your dependence or addiction is an unhealthy one. If it feels freeing, I'd also venture to say your relationship with it is an unhealthy one, but you skipped a step and already have the self-awareness to recognise it as such.

As we will further examine in the final chapter, the reality is that as a society, we consider ourselves bored often, but simultaneously we do not like to not be doing anything that requires too much mental or physical energy. What an ironic position we've got ourselves into!

But that's not all!

These are the mental health issues most people recognise, but the truth is social media may be contributing to the rise of a host of other diagnosable mental health issues as well, such as narcissism, delusion, and two brand new disorders it most likely single-handedly created: FOMO and Selfitis. Consider them Easter eggs we'll find and explore later on...

---

32 "How Much Time Do We Spend on Social Media?" Mediakix, accessed May 21, 2018, http://mediakix.com/2016/12/how-much-time-is-spent-on-social-media-lifetime/#gs.jryzpdk.

FIVE

Most of It Isn't Real Anyway

"Social media has created jealous behaviour
over illusions... Some of you are envious of
things, relationships, and lifestyles that don't
even exist."

– Unknown

We love Harry Potter, but do we let Harry Potter affect crucial decisions in how we live our lives? We love Star Wars, but do we change the way we present ourselves to the world because we let Star Wars make us feel bad about ourselves? No, because Harry Potter and Star Wars are *fantasy*. We know it is fantasy before opening the book or walking into the theatre. That knowledge affects our expectations when we interact with such a book or movie series. Social media is fantasy too, but the scary thing is that we take it at face value, so our expectations of it are different when we engage with it. This misconception is causing us tremendous suffering.

Sure, there's a sliver of truth in social media, but the majority of it isn't real—at least not real in the way that we believe it is. Even if you find someone who isn't filtering the shit out of their selfies or carefully curating their content to exaggerate their lifestyle, chances are they still would never dream of posting screenshots of their overdrawn bank account, spotty back, or evidence of their failed relationships. I honestly don't think I've ever seen or met someone who would transparently display their life 100% on their social media, myself included—and truth be told, I don't think that's even possible. Yes, it's always refreshing to see the odd "no makeup selfie" or the self-deprecating "my house is a mess" post, but those are few and far between. To be fair, why *would* people be 100% transparent? We post what makes us happy to feel good about ourselves. If we only posted the bad stuff, the draw of social media would evaporate. Nobody *wants* to get depressed looking at social media. The irony is that we do end up getting depressed, but social media does it in a much more stealthy, less obvious way.

Most of us are conscious that everything everyone posts is carefully curated, screened, filtered. But I've met so many people who forget it very easily with time. If they were remembering, then they wouldn't be having the emotional reactions they do to social media. Nor would they be putting so much value in what they themselves post and pressure on themselves to "get it right."

Seeing a sexy selfie of someone that's the product of an effective filter plus an extensive Instagram photoshoot to achieve the perfect angle is one thing. Seeing a stream of such images on a daily basis, crowding our consciousness, makes it exponentially worse. The frequency and the amount of consumed information is potentially the "enemy" here. Something seen or heard enough times will reshape our beliefs and behaviours. Imagine someone who scrolls through their social media and chooses to follow a collection of models with a certain body type. This person is bombarded with these images dozens and dozens of times per day. How do you think this shapes how they feel about their own body? How do you think this affects their aspirations for their own body? Maybe this person is out of shape and could perhaps change their body with exercise and diet. But even if they did get in good shape and had excellent health, chances are there are genetic features of their body that they could never change without the help of plastic surgery. So, how is this person ultimately left to feel?

Body shape is just an example; this also applies to lifestyles, money, travelling, and family. We *can* find inspiration on social media, but that same "inspiration" can also remind us of what we don't have and perhaps what we'll never have because we are all beautifully different. Those differences should be embraced.

What makes it all worse is that we end up feeling bad about ourselves over something that isn't even real. We don't have the full picture of the people we follow on Instagram, even if they're our friends.

Online identity does not equal identity.

A lot of people live two lives: the real one and the online one. It is almost like social media gives them a licence to portray what and who they would like to be, compared to what and who they really are. Now I am not necessarily saying that most people are delusional or actively lying— though many are (we'll look at that later!). Misrepresenting ourselves unintentionally is simply inevitable with social media; what we post on social media isn't even 1% of our day. It is just one snapshot of one single moment. I could post a picture of myself all happy and one minute later, receive the worst news ever and end the day being really sad, but no one else would know. They would know only the happy me because of that one picture that captured me in a moment of happiness.

Online identity should never be misconstrued with actual identity. A few carefully selected photos posted in one day is no more a reflection of your identity than three carefully selected sentences you said that day taken out of context.

Often when people are brutally honest on social media, revealing the cracks in their facades, they do it for the wrong reasons—we'll look into that later on. But the majority of social media users, myself included, mostly share only the good, fun, exciting, beautiful moments. Those are the highlights in our lives; they're not the default.

The comparison game
(the least fun of all games!)

> "Social media is training us to compare our
> lives, instead of appreciating everything we are.
> No wonder everyone is always depressed."
>
> – Bill Murray

Come on, admit it! This is a safe space. How many times have you caught yourself looking at people's pictures and ended up feeling a little envious, jealous, and wishing that you could have the same or look the same? If not, then you are one of the lucky few… also, are you human?

Do you know how many times when I'm coaching or chatting with friends they tell me that they don't feel as attractive as they would like or that they wish they had something they don't? Too many times to count. When I ask them to show me what they think is attractive, 9 times out of 10, they will show me people they follow on Instagram or Facebook. Let that sink in for a moment. If they weren't following those people, would they still be feeling the same way? We can't say for sure. But I can say that without social media, those people wouldn't be lying in bed or sitting on the toilet scrolling through image after image of that person reminding them that they look different. What makes it absurd is that what these people on Instagram or Facebook are posting is not real. They're posting the one perfect shot out of dozens of "unflattering" ones, and they may be using a filter that works more magic than Photoshop. That's like beating yourself up because you're not a wizard like Harry Potter! Or because you don't know how to "use the Force" like a Jedi. Holding yourself to standards that aren't even real is completely ridiculous.

The strangest part about social media is that we *know* it's not real. Why? Because we've experienced being on the other side of the coin firsthand. We only post that perfect shot. We use filters that seem to work miracles. We've witnessed how unreal our own photos are. So why do we forget when looking at the photos of others?

Subliminal messaging is no conspiracy theory.

An NYU psychologist, Dr. Lloyd H. Silverman, has been pioneering subliminal messaging research for over 20 years. His findings with over 40 groups of subjects have shown significant changes—often *improvements!*—in behaviour after exposure to specific subliminal messages. In one 1980 study, Silverman used a subliminal message as part of the treatment for half of a group of smokers trying to quit smoking using behaviour modification therapy. One month after treatment ended, 66% of the group exposed to the activating subliminal stimulus were still non-smokers, as opposed to only 13% of the control group. He has reported the benefits of subliminal messages have been observed in assertiveness training classes, adolescents receiving psychotherapy, college students in group therapy, alcoholics in Alcoholics Anonymous counselling, and even in people undergoing behavioural therapy for overeating and insect phobias.[33] According to a 1979 TIME magazine article entitled *Secret Voices,* nearly 50 department stores across the U.S. and Canada were using subliminal messages through their music systems to diminish shoplifting and employee theft. One particular chain reported reducing theft by 37%, amounting to an unbelievable savings of $600,000 over a nine-month period.[34]

The undeniable power of subliminal messaging.

So let's do the math. We spend more and more time on social media and when we do, we are basically bombarded with images of beautiful or fit or toned or rich or seemingly perfect or unnaturally interesting people, lifestyles, places, and items. Then multiply that by thousands of hours seeing that. What do you think is going to happen? What is our idea or benchmark regarding beauty, success, etc., going to become? Again, even if we are super conscious of that, our realities will slowly change. Something that is totally normal by the way, not just with what we see on social media. For example, I came to England dressing a

---

33   "Subliminal Messages Research," accessed May 22, 2018, http://www.deeptrancenow.com/subliminal_messages.htm.

34   "Subliminal Messages Research," accessed May 22, 2018, http://www.deeptrancenow.com/subliminal_messages.htm.

certain way and after being exposed all the time to how people in England dress then of course my taste in fashion changed and I dressed differently. Exactly the same with a constant visual stimuli online.

When we're about to play the comparison game, it's beneficial to attempt a different type of mental gymnastics first: asking ourselves the right questions to avoid getting sucked in to this not-so-fun game. My sister recently gave this a shot. She told me that she'd been to a wedding and started to feel shitty about herself and unattractive because so many of the other guests were thinner, attractive women. Luckily, she had the wherewithal to stop the comparison game in its tracks and ask herself the right questions: "How old are these women? How old am I?" She was a 42 year old woman comparing herself to 20 year old girls. That's never going to go well because it is insane to expect a 42 year old woman to ever look like a 20 year old girl. In fact, it would be a bit *scary* if she did! My sister told herself, "Of course I don't have that body, but more importantly, I used to and now I'm just older." She saved her own day and her own self-esteem by asking those two questions.

So even if you're able to play the comparison game with an image of someone that is in fact accurate (not what we always see on social media), you also need to take into account background, conditioning, and every defining factor that makes you and that other person different. For example, let's say I love going to the gym and I'm working hard to get a six pack and better arms.

Every time I go in, I see another guy there who is *insanely* toned—muscles galore. I assume that he is like me; after all, here we are working out at the gym at the exact same times. So why don't I look like him? Even in this real life circumstance, I'm not taking into account the realities of our differences. The truth is that he could be at the gym for six hours every single afternoon—not just when I'm there—so of *course* he is always going to be there when I'm there. He could be slamming steroids. His job could be fitness modeling. Or he could have absolutely no life outside of the gym—no relationships, no job, nothing... so he's in a position where he has all the time in the world to become that ripped. If this confusion can happen in *real* life, you can imagine how much easier it is for it to happen via social media—especially if you're following a handful of accounts of jacked guys across the world who actually make only 0.000001% of men total. Okay, I'm guessing on that statistic, but still... see my point? If I have time to train at the gym only 3 days a week for one hour, then I need to compare myself to other men who also train 3 days a week for one hour... and who mirror my diet, body type, training routine, and lifestyle in other ways because there are many factors that contribute to health.

Prior to social media, we'd find ourselves playing the comparison game only in certain circumstances where we were already concerned with our appearance, such as at a party or where we needed to show our skills like at that big job presentation. Social media has made this comparison game right in our faces ALL THE TIME. It's not saved for certain events or occasions or places. It's a game we play anywhere, anytime—and so it ends up being everywhere at all times. It's often the way we start our day *and* the way we end it. Does that sound healthy?

Likes And Followers Are Now More Precious Than Gold.

I'll say that again. Likes and followers are now more precious than gold. There are 4.2 billion likes on Instagram per day.[35] On Facebook, the "like" button is pressed 1.13 trillion times per day.[36] Don't think of likes and followers as currency? Well, people are actually spending their money *buying* likes and followers. People even buy views on YouTube. Buying likes and buying views is a common tactic for people (especially those who are running a business) to appear more popular than they actually are… because popularity in and of itself gains… well, *more* popularity. What does that say about us if we're willing to buy the validation we know isn't even real?

This is, by far, one of the most crucial concepts to digest and understand in this book. Reread this section until it sinks in for you and you grasp what the repercussions

---

35 Salman Aslam, "Instagram by the Numbers: Stats, Demographics & Fun Facts," Omnicore, accessed June 7, 2018, https://www.omnicoreagency. com/instagram-statistics/.

36 Salman Aslam, "Facebook by the Numbers: Stats, Demographics & Fun Facts," Omnicore, accessed June 7, 2018, https://www.omnicoreagency. com/facebook-statistics/.

of this are. I must say, out of every facet of social media and its effects on our society, this is probably the thing that mesmerises me the most because I can logically understand how it's happened, but I simultaneously can't understand how we *let* it happen.

More and more people have become new breeds of hunters and fishermen, and they've exchanged the rifles, fishing rods, and nets for one weapon of choice: mobile phones. The modern hunters and fishermen do not look for prey though; they hunt and fish for likes, comments, and followers. Jokes aside, this new behaviour of hunting for something just for the sake of having it is fascinating. Comments and likes do not translate to monetary gain necessarily. They are not things you can possess and hold and gaze upon. They are a digital currency that nobody but *us* deemed valuable. How crazy is that?

I mean, really—what *are* they? What do they even mean? Where do they come from? There are people working overtime and spending *money* to get likes and followers to appear more "famous" than they really are. Unless you have a business to promote, those likes and followers mean... *nothing.* Sorry for the literary bitch slap, but it's true. I witness too many people wasting their lives focusing and getting likes and followers that amount to *zero change in their physical lives.* Think about that. ZERO CHANGE. And those likes and followers sure as hell don't make these people feel better about themselves in the long run—even though they think that they will. If these likes and followers actually did boost everyone's self esteem, then everyone would be so confident within weeks of being online that they'd be out pursuing their dreams and kicking ass—not posting more and more while feeling worse and worse. So what are they gaining? Why do we value likes and followers the way we value *gold* when the two are so very different?

Let's break this down. Call me Captain Obvious, but what is "a like"? It's a double tap on a screen that doesn't even take one second. It requires zero effort. I know this because I've done it. Having done it, I also know that giving something a like also requires barely any thought. Sometimes I'll like something just because... why not?

Years ago, I was in France for Christmas. I was on my phone, scrolling through Instagram. Instagram wasn't big in France back then. My sister wanted to see what it was so she was looking with me. After a few seconds she asked me, a bit confused, "Why do you like pretty much every picture?" I wouldn't go as far to say that I *blacked out* while scrolling, but there certainly was a lack of awareness in my action. It was just a habit. I didn't absolutely *love* every single picture and video that I was liking. They weren't even the nicest things I'd seen in a while. It was just a reflex; I follow their accounts, so I like their stuff. The end.

I am not saying that everyone does that. In fact, I know many people who rarely like any photos. Either way, it shows that people like me who like hundreds of pictures or posts a week don't really *actively care* about the content of those posts. I care about the friends posting them, but liking their posts isn't defining my character so to speak.

In my experience, this resonates with most social media users. We like posts because that's what you do on social media... not because those posts are deeply affecting us.

It doesn't help that most people post the same things over and over again. If you come across someone's selfie, chances are they post many selfies. And more often than not, it's the same people liking and commenting on those posts because that's the interaction they're seeking on social media and they do that on many accounts—not because your posts are particularly moving for them.

To put it plainly: Sophie or Michael, who lives miles and miles away from you, whom maybe you've never even met, who follows hundreds of other people, who likes dozens and dozens of posts while rapidly scrolling through Instagram while sitting on the toilet, does not reflect how great you are or how attractive you are or how anything else you are via her or his likes or comments on your account.

If the joy of posting is limited to the act of posting itself, then you're not depending on validation from other people. You wouldn't need to be notified of the likes rolling in on that post and you certainly would never check to see how many likes it's gotten. But who does that? Do you know anyone who honestly posts with no concern of the response that post gets? I just took a peek at my Instagram feed and the first post I saw was a selfie of a guy I know in bed and shirtless, with a caption reading "Happy Valentine's Day." Surely if the purpose of this post was to wish someone a happy Valentine's Day, there are more efficient ways to do it than posting this. But he didn't post it to spread Valentine's day cheer; he did it for the reaction it's going to get. Right? Or what about the woman taking a gym selfie posing with an unnatural arch in her back to push out all the "right" places with the unrelated caption, "Wow, I can't believe how empty the gym is today!" Or the image of a lone coffee cup in the car, clearly intending to show off the expensive ride more than the £4 latté with the vapid caption, "Need my coffee." Sorry, friend. If any of these people are you, it's nothing personal. I understand how social media has led many of us to this point.

I think there is a way to post for ourselves and exercise moderation within healthy boundaries of this cycle of depending on constant validation. But the first step is simply becoming aware of the obsession and the cycle.

SIX

Are *You* Still Real?

"Being famous on social media is like being rich
in Monopoly."

– Unknown

When it comes to social media, it turns out that being
out of touch with reality is somewhat contagious. It's one
thing recognising that so much of what you see on social
media isn't even real, and it's a whole different thing to
recognise the effects that has on the realities in your *own*
life. I witness way too many people not only forgetting
that the images they're bombarded with daily aren't real,
but also forgetting what is real about *themselves*. And this
isn't a surprise. When we're spending thousands of hours
focused on something that isn't real, it makes sense that
our radar for detecting what's real beyond social media
might go a bit haywire, too.

It's a bit like coming home after you've been on holiday
for too long—reality is a shock to the system. When I used
to work as a flight attendant, pretty much every trip back

from a poor country I'd hear at least one passenger tell me, "I can't believe what I have seen and experienced. This is it—I'm disgusted with this superficial life I lead and I'm making huge changes as soon as I get back." I've kept in touch with some of them, and one week later, they were back to their old selves. I tell you this story to show that as little as one week immersed in a third world culture was enough to deeply shift these people's realities—and then one week back in the first world was enough to shift them back. We are incredibly malleable. Our realities are incredibly malleable. The effects of seeing the world through "social media" glasses may be very different from seeing it through the perspective of a third world country—but the *extents* of the effects for each aren't very different at all. The longer we're immersed in something, the more our realities shift.

I was talking to a friend a few days ago and we were speaking about girls who look really sexy, in her own terms: "girls who look like bimbos." Yes, this label was *positive* for her. She was saying that "ALL the girls" look like that now. As we were sitting in this coffee shop, I pointed out every woman who came in and asked her if each woman looked sexy "like a bimbo." Of the 75 or so women we observed over our time together, there wasn't a single one she admitted matched her description of "all the girls." Of course, I knew right away what was the real issue: my friend was spending way too much time on social media, following women who all looked a certain way, giving her the impression that this was how all women looked now, *and* setting the bar for *her* to look that way too.

There are a myriad of ways social media alters our realities about ourselves and our lives…

False sense of self.

Everybody—and I do mean EVERYBODY—likes to be liked, appreciated, and complimented. That's a normal human desire. When you're on vacation and you're feeling great about yourself in that new swimsuit, you want to capture the moment and post it. Although we know likes and comments have zero actual value, we can't deny that getting likes and comments makes us feel nice! There's nothing wrong with the act of being complimented in and of itself. If it happened organically, meaning you took a photo of yourself *because* you were feeling good, and the likes and comments were just an unexpected cherry on top, then great! You've placed none of your self-worth on the value-less likes or comments themselves.

But social media encourages us to get this progression a bit backwards. We seek to feel good about ourselves for a moment *because* of the likes and the comments. How far are you willing to go for validation? One young woman recently made headlines for attempting to smuggle 77 pounds of cocaine via an Instagram-worthy vacation cruise, "partly doing it for Instagram likes."[37] Um… the

---

37 Michael Bartiromo, "'Cocaine babe' tells court she smuggled drugs for 'likes and attention' on Instagram," Fox News, accessed May 2, 2018,http://www.foxnews.com/travel/2018/03/22/cocaine-babe-tells-court-smuggled-drugs-for-likes-and-attention-on-instagram.html.

struggle is *real*. Okay, most of us aren't trying to smuggle inordinate amounts of cocaine anywhere, but *many* people go out of their way to stage those "moments" in the hope that the likes and comments to come will *make* them feel good about themselves. This isn't organic, so it's certainly not honest. And perhaps the reason we end up feeling icky again even after all the likes and comments is because we know deep down that it was, in a sense, a lie. Still, we're unable to get out of that cycle of posting contrived, dishonest snapshots of our lives because social media trends encourage it. Like a drug, people become addicted to the momentary validation that feels good at first, but makes them suffer in the long run.

Have you ever posted a picture and when you don't have enough likes in X amount of minutes, you've deleted the picture? If you have never done that, there are plenty of people who have and who continue to do it regularly. This behaviour demonstrates how backwards we've gotten that healthy progression, and it leads me to ask these three questions:

1) Are you posting things on social media for yourself or for others? If you use your social media platforms to post what you're *already* proud of, then why should it matter what others think?

2) As we discussed earlier, likes mean absolutely NOTHING in most cases. So bearing that in mind, will a number of likes truly change your day, your month, your *life* for the better?

[71]

3) What fulfilling, meaningful things are you *not* doing with your time that allow you to hang on your phone all day counting how many likes you're racking up?

How honest are you being with yourself? And how honestly are you representing yourself?

The mask of social media encourages multiple personalities.

That last question leads into another more specific issue of false sense of self. I have met too many people who are super shy in person with very little to say, but *aggressively* outgoing on social media. Many of these people seem to be bravest, most vocal, most opinionated, and most selfie-centered online. The disparity between their double personalities is huge. But honestly, social media encourages it, doesn't it? It's too easy to be someone you're not when you're online. Remember how we talked about how cyberbullies would never say a fraction of the cruel things they say online to someone's face? Well, that phenomenon applies to more than just insults. People become more outspoken in all ways online, foregoing all courtesy and even empathy. And for *what*? Being outspoken is by no means necessarily a virtue, so why does everyone seem to write off this social media trend as being okay?

Still don't believe me? If you're at all familiar with dating apps, then maybe you'll see my point. As I'm also a dating and relationships coach, I've seen countless scenarios where someone is hitting it off by chatting with someone online, and then meeting them in person only to be shocked by the difference. It's easy to be a different person on dating apps; all you need is one exceptionally good photo of yourself and a quippy profile that could have been written by anyone. Plus, you have all the time in the world to think of the perfect replies to those texts—very unlike a real conversation.

False sense of being social.

How comical is this? It is called social media, but too often it either makes people be unsocial or gives them a sense of being social when, in fact, they are not at all. As a coach and active observer, I've witnessed this strange dichotomy between people who feel extremely lonely and isolated, yet they're extremely "popular" and active online. They truly live their social lives online: commenting, liking, "meeting" new people. How can there be such a disparity between the two—Mr. or Ms. Popular online, but feeling friendless in real life? What makes the problem worse is not making the connection that these two could be related. These people think, "I have so many followers and online friends, but I have no people to open up to face-to-face." This makes them overcompensate online, becoming even more active, and the vicious cycle is strengthened.

It may sound obvious, but it's worth explicitly saying: being friends on social media has nothing to do with being true friends. Real friends support each other, make time for each other in their lives, make sacrifices for each other, and much more. You can't really do any of these things on social media. It's easy to "support" when that support just means… a comment. That's not friendship.

I recently noticed a status posted by a girl I know at the top of my Facebook feed that read, "I have zero social life." This girl is *always* on Facebook. She's posting selfies, updating her status, and "engaging" with others constantly. Is it a coincidence? No. That status and her behaviour are integrally linked.

One of my greatest pet peeves is spending time with someone who I *do* consider a friend, only to have them on their phone the entire time we're together. It's rude, disrespectful, and communicates to me that our friendship is not worth their focus. The subconscious messaging we communicate to those around us by being on our phones can be just as damaging as actually being on our phones. It is details like these that shift our reality.

Social media "friendships" require far less work… and are far less strong.

Piggybacking on what I touched on in the last point, so many people confuse real, deep, meaningful friendships and the illusion of having lots of friends by being popular online. It's nothing more than simple math: we only have so much time in the day and so much energy to spend on other people. If we use all we have in escrow on social media, there's nothing left for the relationships that actually matter. The longer we spend looking at our phones, the less time we have to look at the people around us.

Social media "friendships" require minimal effort. Well… have you ever gotten a lot out of something you put very little into? "You get what you give" is a common saying for a reason: it's true. All relationships are work. They require time, patience, kindness, openness, communication, compromises, and more. If we don't water them with these social currencies, they wither. And hey, withering is a natural process too—it just separates the relationships that mean something to us from the ones that don't. Ever gotten into a heated Facebook debate with the friend of a friend? Ever pour time and effort into getting a single like from someone you admire on social media? How did either of those things ultimately enrich your life? I've experienced both, and I can't say they did much for me. Spend your social currency on the people who mean something to you. Not the ones who will never be more than an avatar.

Something else worth touching on here is the lost art of conversation. Okay, maybe it's not *lost* yet, but I fear we're losing it. I'm not just talking about the conversations you have with another person. I'm talking about the cultural conversation, societal conversation. The dialogue that underscores our lives. While media continues to grow smarter in many ways, *some* TV programs seem to be getting dumber and dumber, and magazines and newspapers focus more and more on celebrities and meaningless trends. It's very à la film *Idiocracy,* which is a comedy, but its message feels dark now seeing as it seems we're headed in that direction in reality (watch it!). People value more and more their looks and the quest to defy aging. It's much harder to have meaningful conversations—whether with loved ones or strangers— when it's all happening online.

When social media replaces real conversation, it hurts. I was chatting to a guy on my ice hockey team who just had a birthday, and I asked him if it was a good one. He said it was alright, but the worst part of it all was that none of his kids had called him or even sent a card. They sent him a short message on WhatsApp or posted "Happy Birthday!" on his Facebook wall. Getting that response from a random Facebook friend is normal, but from your own kids? We're blurring our digital reality and our physical reality. I've been guilty of this before, and hearing this guy talk about it made me feel bad. Some might call this the evolution of communication, but evolution has no concern for morality. We might be creating new behaviours, but labeling them "evolution" does not mean they're good behaviours.

Rather, this kind of communication is what makes people feel disposable. It also makes us view other people as disposable. When they're not standing there right in front of us, they're not three-dimensional and we lose sight of the fact that they're living, breathing beings with a myriad of emotions, thoughts, and beliefs. The same way we swipe left on a person in a dating app, we swipe left on "friends" via social media daily by simply allowing this medium to make us forget that there's a human soul at the other end of the keyboard.

A few solid best friends and the ongoing dialogue they bring are enough to last you a lifetime, if you're lucky enough to find them and you're hard-working enough to put in the effort.

Our decisions reflect our true identities.

Before the internet, we'd get advice from chosen people we sought out, whose opinions we cherished. Today, we post on Facebook and just see who responds. Then we take their advice to heart and let it truly affect us. Does this help us make decisions that are aligned with who we really are?

I see so many people making a public announcement regarding a problem or dilemma that they might have, broadcasting it to the world, hoping to get some help/ advice/reassurance from their Facebook friends or followers. Maybe they're honestly seeking advice, but bear in mind that many people are also seeking attention and validation through their social media accounts. This means that, firstly, these people may not necessarily be honestly portraying the true scope of the problem they need help with, and, secondly, the advice they get is going to be from loads of random people who are likely nowhere near as compatible with them as their closest friends and family members.

Could someone make a decision based on their desire for validation from followers? Definitely. I've seen people do just about everything for the sake of their followers. But much like people-pleasing, if we shape ourselves around others' thoughts about ourselves—especially when those others are people who do not know us or have our best interests at heart—are we shaping ourselves into *different people?* Are we honouring who we really are?

False sense of belonging.

We end up spending so much time on social media, interacting with more or less the same people, doing the same things all the time, the same routines, we easily end up feeling like we're part of something. Social media makes the whole world feel like a compact community in the palm of our hands. And with community comes the sense of belonging. And when people do not have close friends or family to talk to, it becomes *the* community. We access it with the tap of a finger! Instant community! But… is it really?

Would people actually even notice if we came off social media? Would they attempt to get in touch with us and ask us if everything was alright? There might be a few, but those would likely be the people we are actually good friends with in real life. Social media has this miraculous way of making us feel like an important, appreciated, valuable part of something when in reality, we are just one of a billion social media users. We're just as much an integral part of the social media community as we are of the world. Being a part of the world is obviously great, but it's no intimate community. You can be part of the world and still feel like you don't belong.

A false you?

Check out this fun (and perhaps over-simplifying) formula:

> *[the belief that social media is fun escapism] x*
> *[what I choose to see] x [how often I see it] =*
> *my reality*

If you don't like your reality, then change the formula. Trade out the influences that aren't important to you for ones that truly are—ones you're proud to say define you. We all have influences that define us. What are yours?

This isn't just some hippy-woo-woo shit. Psychotherapists and neuroscientists alike have spent their lives studying how our thoughts create our realities. We're only just starting to see scientific proof of how our perceptions and beliefs directly shape the physical world around us thanks to quantum physics. In his TED-Ed talk,[38] Chad Orzel explained how scientists have performed many experiments trying to determine whether the basic building blocks of our Universe are waves or particles. Each scientist was coming up with differing results, so they argued and argued until they took a step back and questioned the very nature of their experimenting. They discovered that the fundamental building blocks would *become* ether waves or particles depending on the expectations of the scientist conducting the experiment. If that scientist expected them to be waves, they appeared as waves. If the scientist expected them to be particles, they appeared as particles.

The thing is—these scientists may not have even been aware of the fact that they had expectations in the first place. They could have been subconscious. So even if you're not conscious of the way that social media is affecting your thought patterns and beliefs about yourself and the world, it could still be playing a massive role in shaping your world depending on how you use it.

Think about it in a very simple way. Have you ever noticed that when you just buy a new car, it seems like you suddenly see that car everywhere? It's suddenly on your radar and it could feel like your reality is now one in which everyone has the same car as you. This is a form of crafting your reality in a way that is rooted simply in awareness.

---

38   Chad Orzel, "Particles and Waves; The Central Mystery of Quantum Mechanics," TEDEd video, 4:52, https://ed.ted.com/lessons/particles-and-waves-the-central-mystery-of-quantum-mechanics-chad-orzel.

If all that you follow on social media isn't real, then how do you shape your reality? You'd think that your reality would then become that of someone who is diagnosably insane. And maybe it is. Maybe social media has introduced a new form of insanity to all of us: attempting to create our realities with materials that are unreal. It can't be done.

A recent study examining 1,000 girls ranging in age from 15 to 19 found that 63% considered their ideal profession to be "glamour model." One quarter reported that they thought lap dancing would make a good profession for them. Only 4% chose teaching.[39] Oversexualisation is running *rampant* throughout our cultures—and there's a whole chapter on that to come. But setting the absurdity of this sexualisation of kids aside, what do these statistics communicate in a larger sense? Certainly neither their parents nor their schools are likely all communicating to these kids what they should aspire to be. So what is shaping the very goals that drive them? Hint: a large component of that answer is what this entire book is about.

---

39 "Sexualisation of Young People in the Media," Zero Tolerance, accessed May 2, 2018, http://www.zerotolerance.org.uk/sites/www.zerotolerance.org.uk/files/files/SexualisationBriefing_ForDownloadV1.pdf.

SEVEN

The Illusion of Separateness

"The greatest tragedy of human existence is the illusion of separateness."

– Albert Einstein

Einstein was a genius on more levels than one. His incredible insights may have seemed centered around physics on the surface, but below they applied to the greatest mysteries of existence and our spiritual evolution. Perhaps nothing is as detrimental to our evolution as the belief that we're all separate, rather than what we truly are: Alike.

Everything we've talked about so far feeds this "illusion of separateness"—becoming antisocial, obsessively chasing a valueless currency, and constantly playing the comparison game. All these things reiterate that we are not One, and according to many spiritual and intellectual leaders, this reaffirmation is what keeps us living in dischord and not utopia.

No matter what your "big" beliefs are about human existence, it's tough to deny that all of these dividing habits and behaviours are bad for us. Whether you're Buddhist or atheist, divisiveness is always frowned upon, and that seems to be something we humans just know inherently. Sadly, there are plenty more consequences of social media that help uphold this illusion of separateness and ultimately divide us. They slide beneath the radar because of the false sense of connectivity and belonging that social media creates.

Everyone gets a voice—including morons.

> "Never argue with an idiot. They will drag
> you down to their level and beat you with
> experience."
>
> – Mark Twain

One of the most wonderful, beneficial parts of social media is that it gives a voice to everyone. We're better able to hear the stories of marginalised groups of people fighting for change because of it. But this, like many social media features, is a double-edged sword. Everyone does get a voice—including the hateful people who might not have such a platform otherwise.

Don't get me wrong—I believe that everyone deserves freedom of speech! But when we forget to take social media with a grain of salt, knowing that there are people on it who are only seeking to hurt and divide, it can be incredibly damaging. I'm sure you've witnessed it on Facebook for example; some people just want to fight for the sake of fighting.

Social media gives us access to more beautiful, positive voices than ever before. But it also makes racism, homophobia, sexism, and prejudice of all kinds more ubiquitous than ever. It's tough to keep yourself away from that negativity when you're online… it's everywhere. Perhaps this is ultimately good—because shedding light on the existence of darkness makes everyone aware that it's there and that we need to actively change it. However, some people don't process it as well as others—especially kids—and let it shape their own worldviews instead.

Don't fall for the people who just live to write crap online.

The eastern "living in the now" is more trendy than ever, yet we're more *out* of the moment than ever!

I was chatting with my good buddy Gary, and he told me that he went to a concert and pretty much everyone had their phones in their hands filming the concert and watching their screens the entire time. They paid to come and watch a band, see them live, and enjoy the atmosphere. Yet they still somehow ended up watching that band through a screen. Um, what's the point of going?

What was funny about this to me and Gary is that most of them weren't filming to remember the experience. They filmed it so that they could post it to let others know how much they're enjoying their lives. That's what social media has become: painting the picture of the perfect, exciting life you want others to see, instead of just leading it yourself. I mean, we're all guilty of this to some extent. I spent a good three minutes filming Afrojack mixing, but then my phone went in my pocket and stayed there for the rest of the night.

I recently went to a friend's birthday party in a club and I was overwhelmed by how many people spent an inordinate amount of time there just taking pictures, videos, and snapchats instead of dancing, laughing, and truly connecting with their friends. But they *had* to be glued to their phones in order to take enough pictures to get at least a few good ones that would be deemed "perfect" enough for Instagram. That's how this works! Right? The irony is that it's not just their followers who will be viewing these posts and feeling like they missed out. These people may be feeling later on like they missed out, too—because they weren't even present at the party they attended!

Where did real activism go?

When I was younger, my mum worked for a workers' union. She was very vocal and passionate about certain things. I've got to say, one of the strengths of the French is that they do not hesitate to stand up for what they think is right. In France, we love our strikes, protests, and demonstrations! I accompanied my mum to quite a few in Paris. One was against a controversial war, and another one was for Nelson Mandela to be freed. When I got older I went with friends to protest against the government trying to place certain measures on students.

The point is we took it to the street. There are plenty of protests and marches happening today… but if all the people who so vocally protest those things online actually showed up to protest in person, there would have been substantially larger turnouts. The scary thing is that people become complacent because they think they're doing their part by ranting about something on their Facebook profile. Maybe that makes a small difference, but not as much as actually showing up. Expressing our opinions on social media often *keeps* those opinions on social media alone, when they could have a life far above and beyond.

Protesting separately has less of an impact as protesting *together*. When it comes to changing the world, the whole is always greater than the sum of its parts.

It's way too easy to get lost in translation.

Social media is designed to make us feel MORE connected, and yet it opens the door to disconnection like I've never seen. Have you ever fallen in the trap of an endless debate online? Have you had a falling out with friends or family over a post or picture? At the very least, have you ever been upset by a post or picture?

It's so much easier to misunderstand the written word than the spoken one. Why? Because we communicate with far more than just words. We communicate with our tone of voice, our facial expressions, our body language, and the emotion we hold behind our words. People write posts on social media that get lost in translation all the time. Often, the issue gets blown out of proportion. People get hurt, and we end up feeling more divided and separate than ever.

Instead of jumping to conclusions, ask questions to clarify. It will save you loads of wasted time, arguments, and burnt bridges.

The fine line between inspiring and demoralising...

Justin Bieber was found on Youtube. The idea for Starbucks was rejected 242 times before it was born. Bill Gates, Oprah Winfrey, Walt Disney, Michael Jordan, JK Rowling and countless others faced innumerable failures before achieving wild success. As a coach, I am committed to pushing people to fight and work towards their dreams. However, issues arise when people expect too much or have dreams that are too unrealistic, and they're not willing or able to put in the work required. I'm not being defeatist here, but it's important to keep in mind that all those people above are still a very very small minority of the world. There are far more business ideas, professional athletic careers, and artist dreams that failed than the ones that succeeded. So when I meet a person with an average job and an average skill set, feeling entitled to things that are beyond average—without the expectation that they'd also need to *bust their ass* to gain skills and talents far beyond average—I know that person will never be happy because they're somewhat delusional. A nice car isn't enough anymore, we need the super car. A flat or house isn't enough, we need the mega crib. A normal watch isn't enough, we need the the most expensive brand that happens to be trendiest at the moment too. Being a good human being, family member, partner, parent, friend isn't good enough anymore; we want to be famous. It's one thing to dream of the impossible, it's problematic to feel entitled to it and feel miserable when we don't get it... despite having so many other blessings in our lives to be thankful for. I am writing this book thinking there is a chance that it might help loads of people and I really hope it does, but I am not unrealistic enough to expect that it will be the best book ever written.

Winning the lottery is the number one dream for many people. People *aspire* to win the lottery. But can you aspire to something that is just luck? Something that requires no work on your part, except for opening your wallet and buying lottery tickets? Social media tends to perpetuate daydreams that aren't based in work and effort—but are rather lotteries in their own right. For example: the dream of celebrity. People follow stars on Instagram because they aspire to be them. Not because they want to be a singer or an actor or an athlete, but rather because they want to be *famous* or at least have the lifestyle and money to match. But the odds of becoming famous without honing a skill are not too different from winning the lottery. In fact, even if you are pursuing a skill that is your passion and you've worked terribly hard and "paid your dues," the chances of becoming famous are *still* slim enough to be compared to winning the lottery.

Hey, I'm not trying to be a Debbie Downer here. I'm only trying to say that social media can inspire us to want something without following the path that gets us there. It makes us rely on luck instead of hard work and skill. We come to expect our dreams to come true, but really we end up demoralised instead of inspired because those dreams lack substance. They're the dreams that came from social media, rather than from our own hearts.

Again the vicious cycle continues because we want these unattainable things without taking steps to get there, we get further and further from them, and obsessively look at them more and more. This keeps us from living in the moment and actually actively pursuing our dreams. And... you guessed it... this keeps us separate, isolated, and alone in our personal despair.

A word about celebrities and influencers...

When we compare ourselves to that list of people—that minority in the world who have experienced unbridled success—we need to understand that celebrities have lives that we don't have. They have a brand, a persona, an image that they need to maintain and some will be much more "social media active" than others. Many people, myself included, follow movie stars, athletes, influencers and more; there is nothing wrong with that at all. What is so important, though, is to make sure that while following those people, we do remember that they have lives, careers, and schedules that we don't have. Trying to copy their lifestyles isn't a dream, it's a recipe for failure because a) it's next to impossible and b) aspiring towards a result rather than a process will never make you happy. In other words, wanting to have lots of money just for the sake of having lots of money is an empty goal. Wanting to be a singer because you have a gift for singing and you want to devote your life to it—whether you make money from it or not—is a goal of substance because it comes from your love of the PROCESS of singing... not what you'll "get" out of it.

I believe that celebrities and influencers have a duty towards their fans and followers and many are not conscious of this responsibility. In many instances, they are role models of millions and they must make sure that they lead by example, inspire people, and help people—otherwise their influence can be detrimental. Unfortunately, I see too many who probably without even realising, rub their wealth, good looks, and lifestyles in millions of people's faces. I see too many constantly posting photos of their private jets, big cars, and fit bodies that they can *afford* to pamper and make as "beautiful" as possible. That isn't helping their followers who more often than not, simply struggle to make ends meet. In fact, it only reminds them how basic, uninteresting, and poor their lives might be compared to those celebs.

So if you find yourself full of dreams that lack substance and are not rooted in who you truly are and what you can offer the world, think of this: maybe those dreams did not come from you. Maybe those dreams are not even what you truly want, but rather what you've been conditioned to want. Consider this, and then consider replacing those dreams with new ones that you definitely can achieve if you work hard enough.

EIGHT

Living Someone Else's Life

> "Stop wasting time in playing a role or a concept. Instead, learn to ACTUALISE YOURSELF, your potential."
>
> – Bruce Lee

The benefits of social media include the joy of sharing who we are, being proud of who we are and our achievements, and spreading inspiration to loved ones and strangers alike. Each of those are well-earned, and we can be happy in sharing snippets of our lives with friends, families, and others.

I met one of my best friends 14 years ago when I first came to the UK. He has done exceedingly well in life. He started out as a cleaner, and throughout the years, he built a successful servicing company from the ground up. He made this business his priority to give his partner and two daughters a chance to see the world, something he didn't have when he was younger. He's given himself that chance now, too. They travel a lot. Of course with travelling, comes lots of pictures and experiences to share. For a long time, he never posted anything because he was afraid it would come across as "showing off." He didn't want to send the wrong message to anyone. One day I said to him, "Why shouldn't you share something you worked so hard for? Something you completely deserve?" It's not like he wanted to post screenshots of his paychecks. He simply wanted to share fun, beautiful moments from his holidays. That's totally fine. The issue is when people do it for the sole purpose of leading others to believe something about them—oftentimes, something that isn't even true. We run into problems when people post in order to craft a false identity that isn't honestly reflective of their own lives. I'm sure you know people who do this.

We've touched on the different features of a false reality that social media can create. In this chapter, I want to delve deeper into one of them: the lie of leading a double life— your digital life vs. your real life. The truth is this: if you're on social media, you're living a double life—the question is which kind.

The three types of social media illusionists.

1 We are literally all guilty of it, no matter what. Nobody is 100% transparent on their social media because it is *literally impossible to be.* The way social media is designed sets us up for deception, whether it's intentional or not. I

have never met anyone who shares absolutely every aspect (good and bad) of their life! Not to mention it would be strange if they did. But we can agree most people share the good things, because that's naturally what we're *excited* about sharing! It makes perfect sense.

The type of illusionist of this nature isn't an active liar. Rather, it's the digital equivalent of telling white lies. We smooth corners a bit, paint the picture that our lives are slightly more exciting and interesting than they are most of the time. It's unconscious. It's natural.

However, some deviation from this typical formula shows up in some people who are far more conscious of what they post, why they post it, and importantly the *result* they expect from posting.

2 The second type of illusionist covers that deviation of people. Mythomania is a very well known word in France. I'd venture to say about half of social media users are suffering from this condition. What is it?

Mythomania: an abnormal or pathological tendency to exaggerate or tell lies. Someone who feels compelled to make things up constantly could be suffering from mythomania – a psychological condition which leads the person to distort reality, and which, in the majority of cases, is found in people with low self-esteem who seek attention from others.

I have met and heard of so many people who seem to have this. I'm sure you do too. Social media is full of them. This type of illusionist is conscious of their reasons for glorifying their lives on social media. It's conscious action.

Perhaps they're unconscious of the fact that it's a *problem*, but they most certainly consciously put thought and effort into what they post and why they post it.

For example, I've seen people save up their money for years to go on holiday for a single week, live the champagne life, take hundreds of photos, but then slowly post those photos throughout the next year to make it look like that champagne life is their life 24/7.

What is the "why" behind their posts? They lack self-confidence and/or self-esteem and depend upon the validation from the outside world to feel a bit better, to feel a sense of belonging, to feel a sense of worth.

Sadly, more and more people are turning to social media to fill this need. We are a society of increasingly emotionally fragile people; studies show that college students exhibit increasing emotional dependency, anxiety, and depression.[40] Some people might argue nothing has changed, rather people are just finally speaking out about their emotional fragility. Either way, it doesn't matter. The point is that more and more people suffer from low self-esteem, low confidence, anxiety, and stress. We depend more and more on technology to fix us, but it's only a plaster that feeds this vicious cycle.

When these people become slaves to mining shareable content out of absolutely nothing, that's when it takes over their lives and their identities. Without the momentary

---

40 Diane Dreher, "Why Are Today's College Students So Emotionally Fragile?" Psychology Today, accessed June 1, 2018, https://www.psychology-today.com/us/blog/your-personal-renaissance/201508/why-are-today-s-college-students-so-emotionally-fragile.

confidence and self-esteem boosts from their social media likes, they start feeling naked.

3 The third type of illusionist is similar to the second. They are a mythomaniac, but they are defined by their complete lack of awareness. They're not only unconscious of their problem, posting has become an unconscious action for them. They're living in complete delusion.

Sadly, I witness more and more type two illusionists growing into this kind. It becomes more than just about smoothing the corners—they eliminate the corners completely. Their lives become one unnatural, perfectly straight line. I have endless examples of these people in my own life and my work, which makes me believe that this society isn't getting any mentally healthier.

It's more work to maintain the lie than to be honest.

My word, maintaining that lie is like a second full time job. The irony is that working that much towards creating a lie takes up a time and energy you *could* be spending actually making those dreams come *true*. Not to mention the stress of working that hard plus the stress of dishonesty doesn't do your health or your complexion any favours. Research has found that lying less is linked to maintaining better health.[41]

---

41   "Lying Less Linked to Better Health, New Research Finds," American Psychological Association, accessed June 1, 2018, http://www.apa.org/news/press/releases/2012/08/lying-less.aspx.

Digital slavery.

The most effective form of slavery is the kind you place upon yourself because it's more likely to go undetected. No matter how deep you get into your own lies, it's never too late to pull yourself out, be vulnerable, and rebuild a life that's real. There have been Instagram stars who have done this. Essena O'Neill had more than 612K Instagram followers before she quit the platform, calling it "contrived perfection made to get attention."[42] She recaptioned many of her photos with the *truth* behind the calculated strategy behind each post. For example, for an image of her in a tight floor-length dress posing on a gorgeous dock before an event, she recaptioned the post to say, "NOT REAL LIFE – I didn't pay for the dress, took countless photos trying to look hot for Instagram, and the formal made me feel incredibly alone."[43] Then she eventually deleted her 2,000+ posts altogether. She said, "This was the reason why I quit social media: for me, personally, it consumed me. I wasn't living in a 3D world." Her confessions serve as solid proof of the conscious lies and falsehoods behind Instagram and other social media platforms. She was as deep as you could get. So if you get that far, achieve social

---

42   Elle Hunt, "Essena O'Neill quits Instagram claiming social media 'is not real life," The Guardian, accessed June 1, 2018, https://www.theguardian.com/media/2015/nov/03/instagram-star-essena-oneill-quits-2d-life-to-reveal-true-story-behind-images.

43   Mahita Gajanan, "Young women on Instagram and self-esteem: 'I absolutely feel insecure," The Guardian, accessed June 1, 2018, https://www.theguardian.com/media/2015/nov/04/instagram-young-women-self-esteem-essena-oneill.

media "fame," and realise you're in a living hell worse than anything you've experienced, that should be a red flag to all of us.

What makes it even easier to be consumed by this digital slavery is that social media aside, we're still on our phones constantly. It's hard to give up social media without giving up your phone, too. Being so dependent on our phones enables our social media addictions, and keeps us stuck in our bubbles. But God forbid that bubble ever burst because when it does, you could be falling from a fatal height.

Are you consciously choosing your cyber identity over your real one?

Have you seen the movie, *Inception?* There's a part in it that shows a cellar full of people apparently sleeping with tubes running from their arms to machines. These people have traded their real lives for their dream lives. Now, the life they dream is their chosen reality. When they are awake, they consider that reality nothing but a dream. It may be a fictional movie, but it's not an insanely implausible future for us. We've already discussed that as it is now, people spend five years and four months of their lives on average on social media… and even more time doing other things on their phones.

The bottom line is whether you're in a cellar hooked up to a bunch of tubes or you're on your phone for 25% of your life, that time where you're not in your body and not in the present moment is time spent living a life that *is not your own*. How do you feel about that? If that doesn't ruffle any of your feathers, then cool. But it definitely ruffles mine. I'm here, in this body, to live *my* life. I don't want to be wasting time, energy, and intention creating someone else's instead—especially someone else who doesn't even exist.

Whenever you're misleading others, you're always misleading yourself, too...

It's easy to compartmentalise the lies we tell. "I'm fooling others, but not myself." The truth is if you're fooling others, you *must* be fooling yourself to a certain extent too—otherwise you wouldn't feel the need to lie in the first place. Think about that. Whatever is compelling you to lie is rooted in some lie that *you are telling yourself*. "If I were prettier, more people would like me." "If I could afford this lifestyle, I'd have more friends." "If X, then Y." All these false "ifs" lead us to carefully craft and curate our social media identities to get us somewhere where we're not, to make us someone who we're not. But these "ifs" are fundamentally flawed. They're lies we've been made to believe—whether they came from ourselves, someone whose opinion we value, or society.

You cannot lie to others without lying to yourself.

So, if you're interested in self awareness and self improvement, then you have to start with swallowing this tough truth. If you feel stuck already, continuing to do what you've been doing won't ever make you unstuck. If you want things to change, it requires you to make changes yourself.

NINE

If a Society is Self-Centred, Is It Still a *Society*?

"If the whole world was blind, how many would
you impress?"

– Boonaa Mohammad

We've danced around the subject, but it's time to dive right into it. Here we go ladies and gentlemen, I present to you the Oscar winner of social media related problems: narcissism. Narcissistic personality disorder is named after a figure in Greek mythology, Narcissus, who literally fell in love with his own reflection… and died gazing at it because he stopped doing anything else but looking at himself, including eating and drinking.

Narcissism: *Excessive interest in or admiration of oneself and one's physical appearance; inflated ego.*

And what exactly is ego?

Ego: *Your idea or opinion of yourself, especially your feeling of your own importance and ability.*

The difference between self-centredness and self-esteem.

Where most people become confused is the line between inflated ego and self-esteem. Those two things are very different. It's healthy to have good self-esteem and self-confidence; however, it is unhealthy to have an inflated ego. In a particularly poignant article in *Psychology Today,* Lisa Firestone Ph.D. makes the distinction quite clear:

> *"Narcissism encourages <u>envy</u> and hostile rivalries, where self-esteem supports compassion and <u>cooperation</u>. Narcissism favors dominance, where self-esteem acknowledges equality. Narcissism involves arrogance, where self-esteem reflects humility. Narcissism is affronted by criticism, where self-esteem is enhanced by feedback. Narcissism makes it necessary to pull down others in order to stand above them. Self-esteem leads to perceiving every human being as a person of value in a world of meaning."[44]*

---

44   Lisa Firestone, "Self-Esteem Versus Narcissism," Psychology Today, accessed June 1, 2018 https://www.psychologytoday.com/us/blog/compassion-matters/201206/self-esteem-versus-narcissism.

So where does social media fall on the scale? It has the potential to drop us towards either extreme. It *can* boost self-esteem for sure. When? The posts where we're using social media as a tool to spread awareness about a cause that's important to us, to share our visual artwork that makes us proud of our skillset, or to express honest gratitude and admiration for others important to us. Each of these posts support the values Dr. Firestone lists above as being associated with self-esteem.

On the flip side, social media also has the potential to feed narcissism. When? The posts where we use social media as a tool to humble-brag about the blessings in our lives, to gain positive feedback about our appearance that validates our internal value, or to arrogantly proclaim that our way is the right way.

Social media offers potential, but we can't peg all the blame on it 100%. The introduction of social media merely gave voice to behaviours that were already very present, and then became a vehicle to amplify that behaviour.

I've got some tough love for you in this chapter, but don't take it personally. We've all fallen victim to the ego-feeding effects of social media—myself included. What matters is whether or not you still want to be victim or if you'd rather step outside of it.

The *why* determines if it's narcissism or self-esteem.

It's your social media account. You have every right to post tons of selfies, every meal you eat, every outfit you wear, documentation of your gym progression, how many Christmas presents you get, and every night out you have. However, when you're posting such things quite often, the question that's important here is: why do you do it?

When people post these mundane, self-focused moments of their lives, many don't really ask themselves why they're doing it. It's almost like it's autopilot. Sometimes I'll ask a person *why* they posted a picture of their haul after a shopping spree or of the many brand name bags slung over their arm, and that moment is the first time they've ever really thought of it. They end up unsettling themselves with their answer because there's often no logical answer that reflects well upon them. To show they spent a lot of money? To show off the cool new things they got? What other logical reasons are there? So then they're forced to look beyond the logical answer to the emotional answer, and they don't like looking there either because they're then face to face with their emotional wounds that have led them here.

The hard truth is this: nobody cares about the photo you posted as evidence of your shopping spree. That content is *so mundane*. And yet, that photo was posted, so *someone* had to care about it. And that someone is *you*. So the question to ask is: why do you genuinely care about the photo of a shopping bag? What lies behind that action? In this case, it may be a photo of a shopping bag, but that's just a placeholder for the countless other mundane, self-centred, and uninteresting things we post on our accounts.

> "Never has a generation so diligently
> documented themselves accomplishing so little."
>
> – Unknown

Self-promotion for the sake of self-promotion.

When you're promoting a business, a website, and/or a project, you have an end goal in mind. You're taking steps to get closer to that end goal. Social media has brought to light (the *limelight*) a new brand of self-promotion: self-promotion to no end. It encourages simply the general promotion of the self for no specific goal or reason. Nobody has ever considered bragging to be a particularly admirable quality, and self-promotion for the sake of simply self-promotion seems to be nothing more than that. So why do we see it differently than we do bragging? Because we've normalised it!

Only you can determine whether or not your posts are self-promotion for the sake of self-promotion or for something else. There's nothing wrong with sharing pieces of your life that happen to reflect well on you… but always ask yourself *why* you're sharing each piece.

Promotion used to be a word reserved for marketing *products*. Now, it applies to ourselves—which means we've made the self into a product in itself. We promote ourselves now the way that we promote inanimate objects. We market our lives as if they're something we're trying to *sell* people. And why? Why do we need to sell others on something personal that should be very much our own? I don't have all the answers, but I think asking the questions is sometimes enough to provide us with visceral reactions to give us clues to what is right and wrong for us. Asking these questions can also incite spontaneous positive change and growth in ourselves. To me, spending your life trying to sell it to others as opposed to simply living it yourself does not sound like much of a life at all.

Whether you have a business or not, it's good to have an honest discussion with yourself about what it is exactly you're promoting with your social media account. I've seen countless people claim they *need* their profile a certain way because it's for their job... But as an unbiased third party, I can easily see that's a lie they tell themselves to excuse their behaviour on social media. Their "business" doesn't really *need* a constant stream of self-gratifying selfies. We're just brainwashed to think that that's what businesses do need now, because social media is a business in itself and it's capitalising on these lies we tell ourselves.

Selfies, you all look the same.

They all look like… you. And your followers only need to see one photo of you to know what your face looks like! Many social media users have a bad case of selfitis, which is now a diagnosable mental disorder. Seriously. Now classified as a genuine disorder by the American Psychiatric Association,[45] selfitis is the obsessive compulsive desire to take photos of one's self and post them on social media as a way to make up for the lack of self-esteem and to fill a gap in intimacy.

First, the disclaimer: there's nothing wrong with posting a selfie every once in a while. Just like there's nothing wrong with a glass of wine or an occasional lottery ticket purchase. The trouble enters the equation when you lose your grasp on *moderation.* There are plenty of good things that when taken to an extreme could become potentially bad. Posting the occasional nice photo of yourself is, well, nice. Your friends who follow you like you—that's why you're friends! They like to see their friend happy! And for the numerous other strangers who follow you, sure, maybe they like to see you smiling too. However, does it not become a bit strange if you suddenly BOMBARD your followers with selfies? Honest question: what is the value in that? Do you believe you are so beautiful that we'll be happy to see your face as much as possible? Even if you were the most beautiful person in the world, I don't think most people would want to be bombarded with images of

---

45   J. Griffiths Balakrishnan, M.D. Int J Ment Health Addiction (2018) 16: 722, accessed June 6, 2018, https://doi.org/10.1007/s11469-017-9844-x.

you 24/7. Is the Grand Canyon beautiful? Yes. Does that mean we want to look at pictures of the Grand Canyon multiple times per day? No. See my point?

What makes it worse is that the folks who suffer from selfitis seem to believe there is variety in their selfies, but there's really not. Their face hasn't changed in the few hours since their last selfie post. Perhaps it's a different facial expression and a different filter, but it's the same face. It's the same content over and over and over again.

Earlier today I scrolled past a selfie of a girl sitting in front her mirror, trying to look sexy, with a Snapchat puppy ears filter on, and the caption "chillin' after work." That was the third post of her face that day. My question is: WHY? We can't deny this is obsessive behaviour, yet we rarely question it or even label it as strange.

Filtering the f*ck out of selfies isn't that different from lying on your resumé. What do you do when you actually get the interview and you must *be* that lie face to face with someone? When you present a fake version of yourself over social media, how do you feel when meeting the friends who follow you in real life? Or when meeting your date you met over Bumble? Be careful; soon we'll be getting sued for false advertising of *ourselves*. What do we gain in doing this? What is the advantage in presenting a false identity that can easily be disproved upon meeting in the flesh? It would be like posting photos on Tinder of myself with long, luscious locks of hair, going on a date, and then whipping my wig off before getting in bed. What would I have gained with that? Nothing but a few hours of feeling validated for my full head of fake hair. And it ultimately could be wildly counter-productive.

The scariest part is how this behaviour is normalised to the degree that we're unable to see the hypocrisy in our own lives. I recently read a Facebook friend's status expressing her disappointment with how men seem to only be into women constantly posting oversexualised images of themselves on their social media accounts. Want to take a wild guess at what her social media account looked like? She had posted a whopping 530 Facebook profile pictures total and roughly 90% were "sexy" selfies. That's 477 selfies. And yet, here she is complaining about something she deems problematic, without being able to see her inherent contribution to that very problem. When we get so deep in social media that we lose this kind of self awareness, we enter dangerous territory.

This behaviour does not make us feel any better about ourselves. Posting constant selfies is an addictive problem that is now a medically diagnosable illness. Yet here we are, continuing to do it and hoping to somehow feel better.

We rely too heavily on visuals.

Can you imagine what social media would be if there were never an option to upload pictures? What would that kind of social media consist of? It's hard to imagine because so much of what we value has become *visual.*

We live in a visual era. The longer we live, the more technology advances, the better digital entertainment becomes, the more incredible things we have to *look* at. However, does this growing emphasis on visuals end up sacrificing our value of things that can't be seen? For example, having a great sense of humor, cultured life experiences, and an overwhelmingly kind personality doesn't necessarily show up on our visual radars. When we're approaching the world eyes first, it takes longer to see the beauty and value in things that aren't visible.

Considering our narcissism-enabling culture, it's also easier than ever to become obsessed with our *own* visuals: how we look. I live in Milton Keynes, not too far from London. I have been in the UK for a little over 14 years. When I first arrived, I wanted to join a gym and found there were about four in the area. Now there are more than 20. Sure a portion of that is due to growing awareness of health, but come on, the vast majority of people young and old care a *lot* about how they look and not a bit about, say, their cholesterol, viral load, or heavy metal toxicity. If the stiff rise in gyms was all about health, then there would also be a sharp decrease in tanning, plastic surgery, alcohol consumption, and more—which are all very bad for your health as well. Guess what. There's not.

I've seen people go from no exercise whatsoever to sudden training five times per week. The reason isn't a sudden concern with health. I used to know this guy who trained at the same gym as me. He would always come to me and point out the guys who were on steroids, telling me that it pissed him off, that they were cheaters, that it wasn't real. Life got busy for me, and I took a break from the gym for about six months. When I came back, I ran into this same guy and he was suddenly The Hulk. He was massive and also had some tattoos that he didn't have before. I asked him why he changed considering his criticisms earlier. He told me that he was fed up with the fact that every time he would go out, he wouldn't really get attention. The bigger guys with tattoos always seemed to get more of it. I asked him if he was getting more attention now, and he said, "Loads more."

That's a sad truth, but it's further proof that we're not only more visual than ever, we're normalising visual appearances that are not even natural.

Do you *want* your greatest pride and joy to be your looks?

If that's a yes, then great. Your daily actions are likely already aligned with your priorities. However, if your looks are not what you want to be most proud of in your life, then consider this: we only have so many hours in a day and so many years in a life. Time is precious. How you spend your time is what reflects on what you prioritise the most. I have countless clients who say they have dreams of doing this or that, but the way they spend their time tells me something else—as do their social media accounts. Your Instagram profile is a reflection on you and your values, whether you like it or not. Look at yours and ask what story it tells. Is that what you'd like to be your legacy?

Some kinds of attention are better than others.

Getting the wrong kind of attention is a theme that comes up quite often in my experience examining people's lives. Of course, social media plays a big role in this, too. Why? Because we're more than ever visual creatures, and we use social media to create images of ourselves that just aren't true. If those images aren't true, then do they likely align with our true values? Um, no. This means we get attention for things that we don't care about deep down or care about for the wrong reasons, thereby getting attention that is not the kind of attention we want.

If I go to someone's Instagram profile and all I see is photos of beautiful buildings, I logically conclude they must be passionate about architecture. If I go to someone's profile and all I see are selfies in which the person is trying to look really sexy, I logically conclude that this person cares about sexual attention and interest. And yet, I've heard countless women say "I always attract the wrong kind of guys," and men say, "Girls keep thinking I'm a player." Nine out of ten times, I look at their profiles and think "No wonder."

Remember the guy at the gym who turned into The Hulk? Yes, he told me he started getting loads more attention from girls, but he went on to say that none of these girls had personalities or mindsets that he clicked with. If he wanted a girl to appreciate what's in his head or heart though, then perhaps he should have spent more time communicating that visually—rather than spending time crafting his primary visual message: ripped muscles.

So, back to the question that launched this chapter...

If a society is self-centred, can it still be considered a "society"? A society is an aggregate of people living together in a more or less ordered community. But there is nothing more isolating than narcissism. Narcissism divides society, thereby dividing a community into a collection of individuals that aren't *together*.

In its very worst form, social media enables the very worst: boosting narcissism while simultaneously draining self-esteem. That's a double-whammy.

TEN

Oversexualised and Undermined

"I got really offended when my single 'Smile' got banned [during after-school hours] from MTV in the U.K. because it had the word 'fuck' in it. They said, 'We don't want kids to grow up too quickly.' But then you have Paris Hilton and the Pussycat Dolls taking their clothes off and gyrating up against womanizing, asshole men, and that's acceptable. You're thinking your kids are gonna grow up quicker because they heard the word 'fuck' than from thinking they should be shoving their tits in people's faces?"

– Lily Allen

Full disclosure: this is likely the toughest chapter to read with an open mind. Let me preface it by saying everything in here I have gathered from thousands of conversations and testimonials with clients and friends who are *women*. Take it or leave it, but please don't shoot the messenger.

This chapter has different elements relevant for both men and women. But while the section geared more towards men is on its way, this first part is especially important for the ladies. Why? Because we live in a social system in which males hold primary power and typically dominate in roles of political leadership, moral authority, social privilege, and control of property. Considering this, women have understandably had substantially more pressure on them than men do when it comes to controlling how they dress and present themselves to the world. Of course, everything in this chapter can apply to men too, but men have not bore the brunt of sexism the way that women have since the beginning of time. We see far more oversexualised images of women than we do men because our society is still mostly dominated by *men* and those are the images *they* want to see.

This has become embedded in our normal everyday life. Women have bent to fit the patriarchal mould set before them without even being aware that that's what they're doing, without seeing that they're enabling the very thing that undermines them.

Here's where it gets a little sticky. Surely you know the saying "You can't judge a book by its cover." I agree, but in France we say this with a twist: "You can't judge a book by its cover, but you still know that it is a book because it has a cover." In a perfect world, I believe that a woman should dress however she wants to dress—even if that means no clothes (or *cover*) at all—without ever being harassed or mistreated by men because of that choice.

But we do not live in a perfect world… yet. I sincerely hope that someday we reach a point where there are no men left who make sexual assumptions about a woman based on how she dresses. That *shouldn't* be happening. Unfortunately, our society is not so evolved yet. And those assumptions happen all the time. So women are faced with yet another challenging decision: to show as much skin as they want, but accept that they will draw attention from men that could potentially pose more problems for them OR to dress in a way that supports what they *want* for their lives and fight for gender equality in other ways. You're empowered to make the choice for yourself. I'm just here to relay to you what I've noticed first hand in my clients, friends, and the countless strangers with whom I've had discussions. I'm here to help you connect the dots in your own life. We're bombarded with oversexualised images every single day—they're ingrained in our culture to such a degree that we've normalised seeing them. Women feel immense pressure to dress in certain ways even if it's just to compete with other women. This pressure feeds itself and the issue just gets worse and worse. So whether some of this, all of it, or none of this applies to you, it's not your fault. It's simply a reasonable result of living in our modern society. Awareness is how you can combat the negative effects.

The term "oversexualisation" covers a lot of ground...

In social media, oversexualisation can mean many things. One extreme is more obvious: the image of someone in nothing but a thong or boxer shorts in bed. At the other end of the spectrum, it's the photo of someone fully clothed, but the clothing is revealing and what many would consider "sexy." In other words, oversexualisation has become so normalised in our culture that we're not always aware when we are oversexualising ourselves. A good rule of thumb though: if the overriding impression that eclipses everything else in an image can be boiled down to one word—"sexual"—then chances are there's some oversexualisation at play. And there's nothing wrong with that if that is what you are intending. However, problems arise when it actually was *not* what you were intending to communicate with an image. I rarely hear a man complain about getting the "wrong kind of attention" from women. On the other hand, I hear women complain about this *constantly.* What's that about?

Our choices are never completely our own.

Why not? Because no choice is free from influence. Everything we do is a result of something that has influenced us. That's natural. So what sort of influence do you think we receive from our oversexualised culture?

A kind that's not likely too positive. Whether you're a man or a woman, maybe you find yourself saying now, "I *choose* how I dress! I'm empowered to take sexy pictures of myself! All my choices to be sexually liberated come from ME!" Maybe some do. However, in order for *all* your choices to truly come from you only—without any outside influence—then you'd have to be living under a rock. Our culture has an insanely unnatural, unhealthy beauty standard. It's impossible not to be affected by that. And, as a girlfriend of mine once pointed out, if how you dress *really* is just for you, then you wouldn't feel the need to post photos sharing it with the world to get that outside validation. Here's a story illustrating how that beauty standard is truly malleable—it is *learned*.

I went to Starbucks once and two women walked in with fake eyelashes, hair extensions, swollen injected lips, fake boobs, fake tan, layers of makeup, and their outfits were extremely sexy for an afternoon coffee run—one was even wearing an open vest with no bra underneath it. I was standing behind them in the line. When they left, the three young girls behind the counter all seemed completely wowed by the two women who'd just left. I could sense behind their fascination was a sadness— perhaps a feeling of inadequacy or insecurity that *they* didn't look like those women. I said to them "It's a shame that young girls like you look at girls like that and consider them to be the epitome of beauty." They looked at me like I'd just told them I came from outer space and replied with conviction, "Well, *of course* they are beautiful! Don't you think so?" I wasn't shocked by their reply, but I was saddened. I replied "I am sure they are beautiful to some people, but to me? I'll answer that with a question: do you think those two girls would look the same without the hair extensions, fake tans, and everything else?"

Both groups of girls suffer. The two women whom the three younger ones deemed "beautiful" likely feel trapped into looking a certain way in order to feel beautiful, while the three girls behind the counter feel unnecessarily unattractive for simply being their natural selves. They compare themselves to the two women while forgetting that without all those accessories, they actually likely look a lot more like the three girls do. What irony!

The point here is that we *decide* what is beautiful and then punish ourselves for not looking that way or enslave ourselves to a beauty routine that takes quite a toll on our bodies. To illustrate this point, consider what has defined beauty over the last decades and even centuries…

The changing face of beauty.

In ancient Greece, plump women were the highest beauty standard. In the Elizabethan era, women plucked their hairline to make their foreheads bigger and higher. In the roaring 20s, flat-chested women with no hips and boyish figures were the supermodels of the day. Beauty is subject to *trends* because beauty is subjective. Period. If you weren't susceptible to being influenced by the trending beauty standards of your day, then I would be suspicious of whether or not you were human. Nevermind history, different cultures have different definitions of beauty *today*. Beauty standards in Asia are very different from beauty standards in North America. And don't think this doesn't apply to men. Just in the last 150 years alone, the "ideal" male body type has changed five different times.[46]

A friend of mine recently said to me, "It makes me laugh when women say that they wear this or that for themselves. If they really did, then why don't they wear it at home when they're not seeing anyone?" To be fair, I love to get dressed up in a suit but I wouldn't put on a suit while watching Netflix and chilling. Still, she makes an interesting point.

So what is one of the largest factors affecting the beauty trends we see on social media, TV, advertising, and pretty much everywhere else today?

You're not going to like my answer.

It's pornography.

Our obsession with sexualizing ourselves on social media is rooted in our culture's growing obsession with the porn industry. We are oversexualised and we're suffering because of it. *Now* how do you feel about your social media posts knowing what they're a result of?

---

46 James Gould-Bourn, "This Is How Male Body Ideals Have Changed Over Time," BoredPanda.com, accessed June 23, 2018, https://www.boredpanda.com/male-body-ideals-throughout-time/.

Stats like this can't have anything less than a *colossal* effect on our daily lives...

Men, pay special attention here because this section definitely applies to you more than it does to women (statistically speaking). The sex industry's role in our daily lives is much bigger than you think and it's only grown in recent years. See for yourself. This isn't an in depth study around porn, why it's so popular, or anything like that. The whopping, long list below brought to you by Fact Retriever[47] and List25.com[48] is meant only to illustrate that it's no wonder why we have certain expectations around sex due to years of normalising porn in our daily lives. Unfortunately, when we subconsciously equate what's sexy in real life with what's "sexy" in porn, it's easy to attract attention and relationships that we do not want simply by what we wear and what we do to our bodies. Here we go...

1 The sex industry is the largest and most profitable industry in the world. This includes street prostitution, strip clubs, phone sex, and pornography.

2 13,000 adult videos are produced annually, amassing over $13 billion in profit. Hollywood comparatively releases around 507 movies annually, amounting to $8.8 billion.

---

47 Karin Lehnardt, "81 Shocking Facts about Pornography," Fact Retriever, accessed June 1, 2018, https://www.factretriever.com/pornography-facts.

48 Juan Castillo, "25 Shocking Facts About Porn You Probably Didn't Know," List25.com, accessed June 1, 2018, https://list25.com/25-shocking-facts-about-porn/.

3 The porn industry also makes more money than NBC, CBS, and ABC combined, AND more than The National Football League, The National Basketball Association, and Major League Baseball combined.

4 The porn industry's revenue exceeds the revenue of top tech companies including Google, Microsoft, Amazon, Ebay, Yahoo, Netflix, and Apple.

5 There are as many as 30,000,000 unique visitors viewing porn at any given second of any day.

6 The most searched term on porn websites globally is "teen." A Google Trends analysis found that searches for "teen porn" have more than tripled between 2005 and 2013.

7 Porn or porn related content makes up HALF of all content on the internet.

8 A University of Montreal team tried conducting a study about porn, but couldn't explore their original hypothesis because when trying to create a control group of men in their 20s who hadn't consumed porn, they could not find a single one. The study ultimately concluded that most guys are exposed to porn for the first time at age 10.[49]

---

49   Georgia James, "Research Suggests All Men Watch Pornography," Huffington Post, accessed June 1, 2018, https://www.huffingtonpost. co.uk/2011/08/18/research-suggests-all-men-watch-pornogra-phy_n_930349.html?guccounter=1.

9 There are over 68 million daily searches for pornography in the United States, which accounts for 25% of all daily searches.

10 A new porn film is created every 39 minutes in the United States.

11 20% of American men admit they watch pornography while at work, which coincides with Sex Tracker's findings that 70% of all internet porn traffic occurs during the workday (9am – 5pm).

12 88.2% of top rated porn scenes portray aggressive acts where 70% of the acts are perpetrated by the man.

13 Internet porn in the UK receives more traffic than social networks, shopping, gaming, finance, and travel.

14 In 2016 alone, more than 4,599,000,000 hours of porn were watched on the world's most popular porn site, which breaks down to 23 billions visits.

15 Although 25%–33% of those who watch internet porn are women, they make up only 2% of paying porn site subscribers.

And here are some alarming stats about the *effects* of porn on us:

1 Several recent studies have reported that teenagers from all over the world use porn to learn about real life sex.

2 10% of adults admit to having an online porn addiction.

3 Steven Stack of Wayne State University and colleagues found in their research that porn increases marital infidelity by 300%.[50]

There haven't been enough studies done to measure pornography's effects on our society as a whole, but with these stats, we're all smart enough to guess that the impact has to be significant.

I'm not knocking being sex-positive, which means having or promoting an open, tolerant, or progressive attitude towards sex and sexuality. But sex-positive is different from sex-obsessed. Considering the new recent studies starting to reveal the negative effects of porn, we can't deny that there's something not sex-*positive* about the porn more and more of the world is becoming addicted to. I'd venture to call these effects sex-negative.

The clothes don't make the monk!

Okay, maybe that expression is a bit outdated. Who thinks about monks these days? Nonetheless, the meaning is still

---

50   Steven Stack, Ira Wasserman, and Roger Kern, "Adult Social Bonds and Use of Internet Pornography," Social Science Quarterly 85, (2004): 75-88.

highly relevant: the clothing does not *make* the person. We are so much more than what we wear, how we look, our physical image. However, being a highly visual culture, we're quicker than ever to judge the book by its cover (or lack thereof). In fact, most people develop their first impression of anything new within only seven seconds. If that impression happens to be wrong, well… then it's harder work to change that impression later on.

It is hypocritical to value the visual images in the world surrounding you so much that they affect your beliefs and desires, but then be blind to how your own visual image of yourself affects the world around you.

The issue isn't looking one way or another. Rather, it's our expectations and perceptions that contradict how we choose to look. When what you value more than anything is how something looks from the outside—whether yourself or your partner—it's no surprise to get to a point where you realise what you want is not mirroring what you're getting.

Here's an example. Years ago, a friend of mine came to me with a problem. He was from the same kind of bad neighbourhood that I was from around Paris. He's always been a great guy with a heart of gold. He told me that every time he picked his daughter up from school, people would be throwing him nervous glances as if they were afraid of him. He didn't understand why. I knew why immediately. In those days, he had a shaved head, a big build, and he'd wear a really thick gold chain with a vest, rolled up jeans, and Timberlands. He'd pull up to his daughter's school in a black Audi with black tinted windows.

I asked him, "If you're a parent, you pick your kids up, and you see a muscly guy with big gold chains in a car that looks like he's got something to hide, what would you think?"

Without missing a beat, he said, "I'd think he was a gangster. Maybe a drug dealer."

"So why do you think those people are looking at you like that?" I replied.

He laughed and said, "Yeah, but hang on... I'm *not* a gangster or drug dealer!"

But those people don't know that. They pass judgment the same way we all do. They use the clues they see to make a conclusion about a person. Same would go for a guy who showed up to school in a suit and an expensive car—people would logically conclude he was a successful businessman even though he could *actually* be the chauffeur for one instead. Either way, making assumptions is never good! But it's also a part of human nature that is particularly tough to fight! So instead of trusting others to make the correct assumptions about you, control what *is* in your power to communicate what you want to communicate. You wouldn't turn up at an important job interview wearing shorts and flip-flops because you know it wouldn't send the right message about you... so start thinking about the messages you send when you go *anywhere*—not just the important job interview.

Judgment is not fact.

Perhaps if we were all spiritually evolved angels, we wouldn't be so quick to judge. But we're human, and we're learning. And judgment isn't just arbitrary—we judge based on the banks of data compiled in our brains from years of real life experience. This is normal.

My buddy was bummed about getting "the wrong kind of attention" here. But whether we like it or not, he was communicating something about himself in the way he dressed. He might define a gold chain and shaved head differently than the rest of the world does, but when you're concerned with the attention coming *from* "the rest of the world," then your definition doesn't matter. *Theirs does.*

So, apply this to the growing obsession with the worldwide sex industry. If you post oversexualised images of yourself on your social media account, what snap judgments do you believe followers would make about you? Considering how the extreme oversexualisation of the porn industry (and music videos and movies and the list goes on and on!) are being normalised and are affecting our culture in numerous ways, how do you think people process oversexualised images of women and men on social media? Is it that different from the oversexualised images they see on pornography sites? To the brain, which is only concerned with data collection, no. No, it's not that different at all.

We cannot say that how someone dresses means something factual about them. What we can say is how someone dresses can make others make snap judgments about them. This judgment will dictate how we see them, whether or not we'll choose to speak to them, and how we'll treat them. And we have no control over that.

Do people turn to social media now with the same mindset as when they turn to porn?

No idea. At least not *yet*. But here's an experiment that I've done hundreds of times that's produced the very same results every single time.

I'll ask someone to show me their Instagram account. We'll then single out the pictures posted that are "sexy/sexual"—a bikini or underwear shot, for example. Then we'll single out one that reflects something about who they are at their very core—a photo of the client and family, if family is super important to them, for example. Never even once have I done this experiment where the second photo has more likes or comments than the first. Never. Perhaps moving forward, I'd eventually stumble across an exception to this rule, but still: the majority rules. To boot, the sexy one not only has more comments and likes, it has a *landslide* of more comments and likes. No wonder we get stuck in these provocative pic cycles! They're what get the biggest responses because they're what people are *looking for*. And why are they looking for it? Nothing is proven yet, but I'd argue our growing cultural focus on pornography is somewhere in that answer.

And yet… as we examined earlier, those likes and comments hold virtually *no value*. So what are we doing all this for?

Wasting vulnerability on… nothing.

Considering how liberally and carelessly people give something a "like" on social media, what do those likes on your sexy pic mean to you? Whether you're male or female, people of the opposite gender like dozens of pics similar to yours every day. Many also watch porn and sexual content on the internet daily (especially men). So what is the difference to them?

You're a sexual being. We all are. But you're so much more than that. If it's your defining characteristic, what you've shaped your entire identity around, then more power to you! Bravo for figuring that out! But if it's not, then… what *is?*

And if you want to draw people to you who like you for that defining characteristic, or for who you really are, then save yourself a *lot* of time and suffering by representing who you are on your social media account with posts honestly aligned with that identity.

Personally, I would honestly prefer five people to like a picture of me for the right reasons ("right" being the reasons I *want)* than 2000 for the wrong reasons!

How do *you* feel about the sex industry?

If the stats listed earlier in this chapter were in any way upsetting to you, then perhaps it's time to take a deep look at your social media accounts and identify the ways this huge cultural influence could be affecting you and what you post.

We may make our own choices, but every choice is influenced by things outside of us, things that have affected us. Are you okay with one of those influences being a sex-negative society?

ELEVEN

The Elephant in Your Relationship

I always say a relationship between two people is actually always between three parties: you, them, and society. Both you and your partner could be the best version of yourselves, both working on the relationship, but if either of you let society get in your head via social media or TV, you can end up sabotaging what could have been a perfectly healthy and wonderful relationship. The same way that society has a strong influence on every individual, it can have a strong influence on any relationship too.

Sustaining any relationship, no matter how long it has been going for, whether it's romantic or platonic, is always going to require effort—through all the ups and downs. Knowing we use social media daily and many of us depend on it to fill voids in our lives, a logical conclusion to make could be that social media affects our relationships the same way it affects us. Could it even interfere with the future success of a relationship? Possibly.

I've had more and more clients, friends and strangers tell me that social media is damaging and sometimes even ruining their relationships. Relationships can be demolished by huge deal breakers, such as differing desires ("I want kids but you don't!"), but they can also be just as easily demolished by the small daily issues that add up to *become* huge. Social media is one of those little things that can grow into a big deal.

Why post sexy pics when you're in a happy relationship?

This is an honest question with a few potential answers. Either you're not actually in as happy a relationship as you thought, and you're subconsciously still "shopping." Or because you're still using social media to validate you from the outside instead of gaining that validation from yourself.

Have you ever been in a relationship with someone, seen them post a sexy photo of their legs in the bathtub, and then suddenly felt insecure about the relationship? Maybe not. But you've more than likely see *someone* post the legs-in-the-bath or legs-on-the-beach or any other sexy pic and maybe wondered about that person's romantic relationship. It happens all the time. And it definitely brings insecurity into relationships. And by the way, if you're on the beach, in the bath, or in bed, there is literally no need whatsoever to include your legs in the picture.

I recently saw a picture of a friend in bed with his chest, arms, abs and lower abs all on naked display. This friend also has loads of photos with his girlfriend on his account, so anyone can see he is in a relationship. And yet, the comments under this picture are exclusively from other women: "Yummy," "Looking hot, sir," "Sexy abs." Why do it? Why do we need this constant sexually-charged validation from people *other* than the one person we're actually having sex with? Doesn't it seem a bit backwards?

If gaining this validation on your social media account is more important than building and preserving a healthy, flourishing relationship with your potential life partner, then congratulations, your actions line up with your priorities. But if your real-life relationships are more important, then why do it?

Social media's role in micro-cheating.

A while ago, I was chatting with a friend of a friend and he was telling me that his relationship of a little over a year had been difficult for the last 3 months; more arguments and less sex. He was saying how he found himself more active on his social media, liking more and more pictures on Instagram of other women, and of course without realising it at first, drifting away from his girlfriend. It is just too easy, we are a society that exchange things, gets bored quite quickly and replaces what's broken rather than attempts to fix it; unfortunately social media provides the perfect platform for this.

Micro-cheating isn't new. It is defined as small acts that at first glance seem harmless, but that in reality constitute a small "act of cheating". What's considered micro-cheating is quite broad but not very clear—perhaps it changes from couple to couple. Social media fits into micro-cheating in a variety of ways. According to psychologist Dr Martin Graff from the University of South Wales, micro-cheating can have all the same consequences as a full-blown affair. Checking former partners' social media accounts, sending heart emojis to people other than your partner, and saving the phone number of someone else under a fake name could all constitute as micro-cheating. "It can be something as simple as repeatedly 'liking' someone's posts on Instagram or commenting on someone's Facebook," said Dr Graff.[51]

Does it feel good when your significant other likes a sexy picture of some other girl or guy? No, it doesn't. So is it wrong? Considering all the reasons we've previously examined for why people like those sexy social media pictures, it certainly doesn't feel innocent, and even if it *is* innocent, it still comes across as kind of inappropriate and pointless. For many men or women, scrolling through naughty Instagram pics isn't different from scrolling

51   Shivali Best, "Liking someone's Instagram post is now seen as 'mi-
      cro-cheating' and can DESTROY your marriage," MSN.com, accessed
      June 1, 2018, https://www.msn.com/en-gb/lifestyle/family-relationships/
      liking-someones-instagram-post-is-now-seen-as-micro-cheating-and-
      can-destroy-your-marriage/ar-AAuImxv.

through images on porn websites. Browsing through social media is like endless window shopping. It's easy to create tension and doubt in your relationship if you or your partner is scrolling through social media all the time, liking others' sexy pictures, because it can give the impression of dissatisfaction with the relationship and the need to keep looking—even if it's subconscious.

Sure, in the grand scheme of things, we know that a "like" is valueless, but we also know that we as individuals allow those likes to *validate us*. So by liking a picture of someone else's cleavage, we *are* saying, "Nice cleavage" or "Nice biceps."

Whether you were dating someone exclusively or you were in a serious relationship, would you feel comfortable saying in a flirty way to a stranger "You've got a really hot body... nice arse" with that person you're dating right next to you? Um, probably no. So why do we do that with our likes and comments on social media? Why is it okay online but not in reality? Is it because we don't think we'll be caught? Or because we think it means less? Either answer is troubling.

If we're afraid we will be caught, then that implies we know that social media aids us in deception. It means we're aware of the fact that we are not transparent when we're on social media. And if we're aware of that, then that means we're actively making the decision to choose dishonesty. Is that aligned with the person you want to be? And is it going to help your relationship in any shape or form?

If we simply think giving a like or comment on Instagram means *less* than it would mean face to face, then that's quite hypocritical considering how much value we place in the likes and comments we *receive* on social media. If we're going to give likes and comments very little value, then that needs to apply to likes and comments across the board. That would mean we're not affected by the validation we receive via social media or so obsessed with posting something with the hope that it'll go viral. That would mean we're not guilty of posting back to back selfies ourselves and we don't feel a high when that post pushes over 100 likes.

I would like to think that NOBODY who is in a relationship would tell strangers on a daily basis that they look hot, gorgeous, or have a great body. It's hurtful and not cool. The same way that digital presence enables bullies by masking their identities, it empowers us to say things we'd never say in real life. Point blank: social media makes it easier for cheaters or people already prone to dishonesty to hide it better and have a lot more options. It enables men and women to be assholes by giving them more tools to hide, creep, and cheat. It enables people in relationships to behave as though they were single.

One of the most common situations I encounter when coaching is women who are crushing on men in relationships because they've been led on. How have they been led on? Because they receive private messages, heart emojis, and flirty comments on social media from men who they know are in relationships. I've had *hundreds* of women tell me this. I am sure some men have this problem too, but in my experience, it seems to be mostly men in relationships who are messaging women.

Maybe it means nothing to those men. But it certainly means something to the women they're messaging and it would definitely mean something to their significant others if only they knew.

You look like X, but your partner keeps looking at Y.

Of course it is totally natural to fantasise about celebrity crushes—not everyone can be with Brad Pitt or Rihanna. The problem is that social media reveals information about us that's quite superficial, and then based on that data, we make snap judgments about what they like. The trouble comes when we start comparing ourselves to what it seems like our partners superficially like. Here's an example.

A good friend of mine once told me she didn't feel attractive enough for her partner because she is constantly seeing her boyfriend liking pictures of other girls. She showed me screenshots of her boyfriend's Instagram activity. He liked a lot of pictures of other girls and there was a theme with how all these other girls looked. They were all brunettes in underwear and bikinis, tanned, with huge breasts. This friend happened to be blonde, fair-skinned, and not particularly curvy. Needless to say, she

was beautiful and had no reason to feel unattractive...
other than the reason that her boyfriend affirmed on a
daily basis that although he was attracted to her, he was
also attracted to women who looked nothing like her. No
matter what this girl did, she would never look like these
other women without the help of surgery, fake tanning,
and hair dye, all of which she didn't want to do. It wasn't an
issue at first, but with time, it undoubtedly created doubts,
fears, and insecurities in the relationship.

The sad truth is whether you're constantly looking
at sexy images of other people on Instagram or you're
constantly looking at other people on porn, and your
partner or wife or husband does not match that image of
the other people you're constantly looking at, what are the
chances you're going to stay interested in your partner?
And how is that going to make your partner feel?

Broadcasting your relationship online.

"A relationship should be between two people,
not the whole world."

– Unknown

A friend of mine recently told me that he has zero pictures
of his relationship on social media because he specifically
wants to keep those moments between him and his
girlfriend. It makes them feel more cherished, more
special. He doesn't need everyone to see every date they

go on, every holiday, every kiss. There's nothing wrong with posting something about your relationship on social media, the issue arises when you're *living* your relationship on social media (and everyone else is living it with you).

A study featured in The Atlantic shows that the more someone shares how amazing their relationship is, the more likely it means that there are cracks in it.[52] The same study points to evidence revealing the reasons why many will share how great their relationships are isn't because they are so happy that they want to share it with everyone, it is more because they are looking for the likes and comments, which will bring validation of the relationship itself. I've had others insist to me that they post to reinforce that their partner is *theirs*. And of course, there *is* the option that they're publicising their relationship simply because they're happy and in love and want to shout it from the digital mountaintops.

I am sure different people do it for different reasons. When it becomes worth examining is when you notice an unmistakable trend in your behaviour or someone else's. Are you constantly posting photos of you being affectionate with your partner? Do you post constant pictures of the new person you're dating every time it changes? What do these patterns mean and what do they say about us?

We also see the reverse: people using social media to twist the knife in an ex-lover's back who might have

---

52   Cari Romm, "The Psychology of Oversharing Facebook Couples," The Atlantic, accessed June 1, 2018, https://www.theatlantic.com/health/archive/2014/08/the-psychology-of-oversharing-facebook-couples/376112/.

cheated, overdramatic posts with captions like "If you can't handle me at my worst, then you sure as hell don't deserve me at my best," and the very cryptic posts shared with the public yet targeted at one specific person... and if your followers are friends, they can usually guess who.

Whether you're broadcasting the good or the bad, the question remains: how is this behaviour affecting your relationship? If it's really about the two of you, then why involve a bunch of strangers you've never met on the internet?

But my biggest question is this: Does sharing with everyone what the two of you share alone together somehow make it more special? If not, then take a long, hard look at why you do it. And if it *does* make it more special, consider why your relationship isn't special enough just on its own.

Not in a relationship yet? Social media affects you too.

Let's face it, our social media profile is basically our personal online CV, and if we're not careful, it says more about us than we want it to. So when two people meet and swap their Instagram and Facebook, they're essentially applying for the job of being in that other person's life.

The question we're left with: can you "get to know" someone, after already getting to know so much of them from their social media accounts (especially if that person is the type who posts all the time)? It makes it a lot tougher. It also isn't a completely *honest* way of getting to know someone because, as we've already examined, our social media accounts can't be completely honest in the first place. However, we buy into the illusion and believe we *have* honestly gotten to know this person by swiping through their pictures and reading about 200 words or less on their profile.

There is a beauty in getting to know someone. Meeting them, hitting it off, and feeling like you could talk for hours because you have 1,323,543 questions to ask them. With social media, we're often stripped away of that opportunity because we make snap judgments that prevent such an experience from ever happening.

On the flipside, seeing what someone is compelled to post about themselves says more about them than the content itself. This is when social media is quite helpful in determining if it's worth spending time with someone. For example, if a woman is looking through a guy's profile and all his pics are shirtless selfies of him at Las Vegas pool parties, and the comments are all flirty dialogues between him and other women, she might want to quit while she's ahead if she's looking for something serious because he obviously is not. Or at least… that's what he's communicating with that profile.

I'd even take it a step further. Call me old fashioned, but there's something so electric and sensual about having no idea how someone looks underneath their clothing and then undressing them for the first time. It's a little cheesy, sure. But there is some truth to the power in leaving things to the imagination. When you tell people what it is before allowing them to imagine, then you sometimes eliminate the chance that they'd want to take the time to get to know you and find out for themselves. And since so many people post sexy pics of themselves on social media, it's not just you who already knows how they look underneath their clothes—it's you and hundreds, or possibly thousands, of others.

In and out of relationships for the wrong reasons.

We've already talked about the fact that social media doesn't provide the strongest foundations for friendships and how often the types of "romances" that begin with social media are the type that are relatively superficial. And just as all relationships can start on social media for the wrong reasons, they can end on social media for the wrong ones too.

Our differing behaviour on social media creates rifts between people. Some people are in much more deep than others. The ones who aren't in so deep end up looking at the ones who are in deep and judging them by their obnoxious social media behaviour rather than for who they really are inside. I've known plenty of people whom I've loved spending time with in real life, but their five selfies per day and vapid posts get so annoying that I end up unfollowing them. The people on whom social media has an iron grip are in the most ironic situation of all: they depend more than others do on social media to make them feel loved and connected. Yet social media delivers to them the very opposite by bringing out the worst in them and pushing on their insecurities daily.

Inhuman expectations of the humans around us.

Truth be told, Hollywood and Disney are both guilty of creating these same unsustainable expectations about love and relationships that social media has created. When we constantly feel like we're missing out on some fairytale love that we don't have, it makes us feel like the relationships we do have are valueless. Yet, those relationships are *real.* So we end up worshipping the relationships that are fantasies and sabotaging the real ones right in front of us.

And instead, we end up valuing the image of the relationship more than the relationship itself. It sounds crazy, but I swear I've seen people who just want to get married for the image of being married—it's not so much about the person they're marrying. They want a ring that looks just like this, a slideshow of wedding photos straight out of an Anthropologie catalogue, and boomerang of the first dance lit by DIY mason jar lanterns. This comes from a daily overdose of stardust we get from social media—making marriage boil down to the mere images of the engagement, the wedding, the creative baby announcement.

To expect a fairytale relationship to match is to expect a life that isn't human. Are we here to live perfection? Or are we here to have relationships that challenge us and make us learn more about ourselves and the world around us?

This affects our expectations of friends too, but in a slightly different way. Instead, with online friends, we're left to expect much *less* of them. How many of us would feel comfortable asking a friend from social media to help us move? Or to talk out a deep problem we're having with a family member? Or to come pick us up when the car breaks down? Social media has normalised our friends *barely* showing up to support us. Facebook events make invitations so casual, that it's become custom to check off "Going" to an event, comment that we'll "try" to be there, and then never show up and never explain why. That's... normal now. And yet, the one expectation we *do* have of friends and mere acquaintances alike is a ridiculous one: to simply be accessible online 24/7.

So...

Whether you're aware of it or not, social media is playing a role in your relationship or it's playing a role in your *not* having a relationship, just as it's a silent participant in your every friendship *or* your loneliness.

TWELVE

FOMO—
More than a Hashtag

"That fear of missing out on things makes you
miss out on everything."

– Etty Hillesum

FOMO, the acronym for the "Fear Of Missing Out," may have begun as nothing more than a funny and quickly viral hashtag. However, when applied to social media users who use those platforms as the number one if not *only* way to feel well liked, validated, a sense of belonging, or a boost of confidence, FOMO takes on a much darker meaning. It's not just missing out on, let's say, a party. It's missing out on a hit of the drug that gives you purpose— and when you miss out, you start experiencing the painful withdrawal symptoms.

FOMO brings a whole new dimension to peer pressure. While we were once pressured to *do* things we were uncomfortable with, now the greater discomfort comes from the fear of *not doing*—and it doesn't even matter what the activity itself is. We just feel pressure to be *doing*. Period. The sacredness of silence and solitude is gone… because if nobody witnesses that we were doing something for ourselves in solitude, it's almost like it doesn't even count.

Without social media, FOMO wasn't an issue. Why? Because it was impossible to see what fifty other friends were doing at any given moment in time. We couldn't compare our present moment with the present moment of a superstar celebrity with the mere push of a button. We *didn't know* what we were "missing out" on—and for a good reason—because we were more focused on our own personal "now" and actually living it.

Pressure to post.

The average person has seven social media accounts.[53] And yet the pressure is the same for those using them often or using them rarely. The person who uses them often sees how often other people post, and they feel the pressure to post themselves just to keep up. The person who uses them rarely often ends up feeling isolated and alone like the odd one out, and ends up feeling pressured to join them even though they don't feel the natural impulse or desire to join. Needless to say, this pressure is typically all subconscious.

---

53   Colm Hebblethwaite, "The average person has 7 social media accounts," Marketing Tech News, accessed June 1, 2018, https://www.marketingtech-news.net/news/2017/nov/17/average-person-has-7-social-media-ac-counts/.

Have you ever opened up Instagram, Facebook, or even Snapchat and noticed someone else's post with new features you haven't yet discovered? And then felt the pressure to immediately find out where those features are, use them on a post of your own regardless of whether or not you have anything of substance to share, and then post it just for the sake of being someone "ahead of the curve"? This phenomenon is not uncommon. In fact, I suspect this happened with many people when the Snapchat "sexy dog" filter came out.

Pressure to be available 24/7

A friend of mine once texted a girl he'd just started seeing about something bothering him. With no response twenty minutes later, he texted her again. And again. And again. He became increasingly upset, assuming she was communicating something with her silence. By the end of his stream of texts, he was breaking up with her. The next morning, she woke up to read this whole stream of texts for the first time. She'd unintentionally fallen asleep early the night before because she had been feeling very sick. He made false assumption after false assumption, and ended up sacrificing what could have been a wonderful relationship for it. This perfectly demonstrates the pressure we feel to be available 24/7... because God forbid we're not, and we could lose a say in the direction our lives take.

Constant availability has become an expectation in our friendships, relationships, and even professional connections. People are often shocked if it takes you more than 12 hours to respond. They assume something is wrong. Is that not strange? Can we truly not unplug for even 24 hours without feeling abnormal?

It doesn't help that apps like Facebook Messenger and Whatsapp tell others when you were online last and when you've read their messages. Somehow we've misconstrued accessibility with reliability. If you aren't accessible enough, people feel they can't depend on you. We worry if we don't respond to our friends within minutes, they will move on and speak to someone else instead. We equate "speaking with someone else" with some form of disintegration of the friendship itself. But if a friendship were so easily destructible, what sort of friendship was it to begin with?

Pressure to reveal ourselves.

Openness by definition implies honesty. But is it possible that too much openness could cross a line into disingenuity? Possibly. When the openness isn't organic, but rather forced, we sacrifice its authentic nature itself.

When you have the impulse to post something that shows off the blessings in your life, where does that impulse come from? For my clients, friends, and countless strangers I've interviewed, I find it often comes from pressure after seeing everyone else on social media posting about *their* blessings and achievements. Hell, I've experienced the impulse myself. You'd have to be superhuman not to. But is that influence truly organic? No. The influence to be "open" about the good things in your life does not come from the desire to be vulnerable and honest with your fellow human beings—or from a place of light. It comes from darkness— a.k.a. fear. Fear of being different. *Fear of missing out.*

We end up revealing things about ourselves that perhaps would better serve us if kept to ourselves. Or we end up revealing versions of the truth that aren't quite the truth at all. We end up posting revealing snapshots of our lives, simply for the sake of posting. Not because the content we have to share or the message we want to communicate is a particularly good one.

I have clients addicted to posting as much as possible simply for the sake of "keeping up". Now with the "stories" feature on Instagram, Facebook, and Snapchat, posting for the sake of posting has truly taken on a totally new dimension. Some people post anything and everything they possibly can. There is no discrimination for what is good enough to make their story—walking, eating, drinking, selfies, food shopping, clothes shopping, all shopping, lying in bed, working out at the gym, sitting in their car, listening to music, watching TV, travelling, the list goes on and on and on. Daily, they stretch to make something out of nothing, and waste their precious time on earth in the process. Examples? The girl who posted a fully edited *video* of her own legs in the bathtub, complete with a soundtrack. The dude who live streams his daily workout, which is the same week to week. Or the people posting photos of themselves apparently "asleep" (*how and why?*). All of these examples beg the overriding question of this book: WHY? Are we living our lives for ourselves or to keep our audiences entertained with even the most banal content?

Is it enough to simply live even if we know nobody is watching?

Social media reduces life into pointless competition.

Posting constantly is one constant struggle in itself. Posting *better content* than everyone else constantly is yet another struggle. Healthy competition can be great. It can push you to pursue your greatest passions in life and outdo yourself when you never thought it was possible. But what if we're not talking about something as valuable as your greatest passion? What if, instead, we are referring to a medium that has zero positive bearing on the direction of your life? Like... posting the very best coffee photo? Can it be done? How many ways can a person post a cup of coffee? And who truly cares enough about viewing pictures of coffee to actually even appreciate it?

A Carnegie Mellon study[54] recently reported that there

---

54 Hemank Lamba, Varun Bharadhwaj, Mayank Vachher, Divyansh Agarwal, Megha Arora, Ponnurangam Kumaraguru, accessed June 1, 2018, "Me, Myself and My Killfie: Characterizing and Preventing Selfie Deaths." https://arxiv.org/pdf/1611.01911v2.pdf.

have been 127 selfie-caused deaths in a 29-month span from March 2014 to September 2016, and many injuries beyond that. Most people are more afraid of sharks than they are of selfies, yet a report from Condé Nast Traveler[55] confirmed only six deaths from shark attacks in 2015 and *dozens* of deaths from selfies that same year. Looks like we've got our fears poorly prioritised. We go to such great lengths as *death* to get the best selfie or the best picture to outdo each other on social media. But… for what?

This certainly isn't the healthy kind of competition that stretches our minds and challenges our hearts.

We see ourselves as we see technology: in need of constant upgrading.

If you've gotten this far in this book, you know now that social media often portrays the unattainable or at the very least, the unsustainable. Most people do not have the intention of deceiving their followers, but the very nature of social media makes it impossible to be 100% transparent about our lives. So we're left with lies to compare our own lives to, believing those lies are real.

This nurtures in us a sense of entitlement, and the fear it creates is a fear of missing out on a life we *should* be able to have—after all, we see all these people online who

---

55   Calder Quinn and Brad Rickman, "Selfies vs. Shark Attacks: Which Are More Deadly for Travelers?" Condé Nast Traveler, accessed June 1, 2018, https://www.cntraveler.com/stories/2015-09-15/selfies-vs-shark-attacks-which-is-more-deadly-for-travelers?tw=social.

have that life! Why not us? With this, we're unable to feel gratitude for what we have and live in the present moment. Instead, we're constantly waiting in a metaphorical line outside the Apple Store. Except it's not for the iPhone 18. It's for the newest model of ourselves.

But isn't that something *we* should be creating? Instead, we wait around for social media to tell us who the next best version of us should be. We wait for it to show us what we want and what we aspire to be. Our mindset becomes a mindset of constant *wanting*—which is also a mindset of constantly feeling *not enough*. We want the same thing but better, bigger, faster.

Aspiring to be better is a wonderful thing. Self-growth is important. But it shouldn't come from a place of FOMO or a place of peer pressure. It should come from a place deep in our hearts and souls, and we should acknowledge that it will take hard work to get there. Furthermore, if we're on the right path, then the hard work should feel exciting to us. Not discouraging.

FOMO keeps us in a state of playing constant catch-up.

Social media moves at the speed of light. For fear of missing out, we try our best to move faster ourselves just to keep up. By doing this, we're setting ourselves up for failure each day because it is *impossible* to keep up. IT NEVER STOPS. The social media feed goes on and on and on. We get so caught up in keeping up, that we lose sight of the entire reason for doing so in the first place. And we end up breaking our necks over just trying to keep up for the sake of keeping up.

The irony here is of course that in scrambling to keep up and not "miss out" on social media, we end up missing out on the moments in our lives that actually matter. And this problem just feeds itself because as social media gets bigger and bigger, we always fall further and further behind. The cycle makes us feel worse and worse about ourselves, but we keep returning to the cycle in order to feel better. The poetry in this is honestly better than fiction!

If we don't want to spend our lives in a constant state of catching up, then it's time to step out of the race. We should live life not as if in a race we'll inevitably lose, but rather as winners who've already finished.

JOMO: The Joy of Missing Out.

> "Don't give them the privilege of knowing
> everything about you. Just because it's not
> posted on social media doesn't mean that it's
> not happening or that it didn't happen."
>
> – Unknown

Lucky for us, there's hope. This term has also blossomed into existence, and I like to think it's comes from people who are aware of the damaging repercussions of FOMO via social media. Spiritual leaders and texts of every religion have something to say about the sacredness of both silence and solitude. There is always room for growth there, just as overstimulation and noise distract us from the real value of our lives. Which category do you think social media falls into? Yeah, it's overstimulation and noise.

What's scarier is the very nature of social media continually impresses upon us another damaging belief: that there's only value in doing something if it's witnessed by others. Sure, the ego has always played a role in this when we do good deeds. A part of us wants our act of charity to be witnessed so that we can be patted on the back. But social media has spread this sentiment into actions beyond charity. Now, when we're doing something fun, our ego needs it to be seen. When we're giving love to someone personally important to us, our ego needs it to be seen. When we're grieving, our ego needs that grief to be seen. Now, whenever we're doing things meant for *ourselves*, our ego needs that action validated by being witnessed... or else there's a part of us that feels like it didn't count. Like... we can go have fun at that concert, but a lot of the fun no longer comes from the experience of the concert itself. Rather, it comes from the rush of *posting* about the concert and seeing our followers react to us being at that concert. How strange is that?

I invite you to reclaim your JOY in missing out. Perhaps by "missing out" on some public affair, you actually give yourself the opportunity to *check in* to a private one; one that truly is *just for you*.

We all leave a digital footprint. If you leave so much of yourself in yours for all the world to see, what is left for just you alone? It's very easy to give. It's much harder to take back.

THIRTEEN

A Waste of (Cyber) Space

"Time is precious. Waste it wisely."

– Unknown

According to SocialMediaToday.com,[56] the average person spent 116 minutes per day on social media in 2017. This amounts to about 5 years and 4 months spent over the average lifetime. This time breaks down unevenly across the different platforms. YouTube takes first place, consuming over 40 minutes of a person's day (1 year and 10 months in a lifetime). Facebook users spend an average of 35 minutes a day, equalling 1 year and 7 months in a lifetime. Snapchat and Instagram come in next with 25 minutes and 15 minutes spent per day, respectively. Lastly, users will spend 1 minute on Twitter, spanning 18 days of usage in a lifetime.

If you happen to be one of the chosen few who have a truly healthy relationship with social media, then perhaps

---

56   Evan Asano, "How Much Time Do People Spend on Social Media?"
      SocialMediaToday.com, https://www.socialmediatoday.com/marketing/
      how-much-time-do-people-spend-social-media-infographic (accessed
      June 1, 2018).

you deem those 5 years and 4 months to be time well spent. For the rest of us, that's 5 years and 4 months spent feeling bad about ourselves. That's time we could have devoted to our greatest passions, to developing real relationships, and experiencing the real world we live in—not the digital one.

We often turn to social media to "kill time," when we are in line at the bank or the post office, when we're left with nothing to do while commuting via public transportation, or waiting for a movie to start. But… since when has waiting become so difficult for us? We are so addicted to constant stimulation that we can't bear any silence or stillness for even a few minutes. I find this incredibly alarming. The concept of "killing time" in itself seems problematic to me. We're only granted a finite amount of time here. Why shoot ourselves in the foot and actively kill any portion of that time?

Is the gain of social media worth the time?

Consider this. I have honestly watched over one hundred hours of instructional golf videos. I am in no way knocking the expertise and helpfulness in these videos, but the reality though is that once I was actually playing golf, I would barely remember what I'd watched. I retained only a small fraction of what I'd learned from watching. Has my game progressed thanks to watching videos online? Yes, a little. Has that improvement been worth the one hundred hours spent? No, not at all. I'd also had lots of golfing lessons, and what I could accomplish in an hour with a coach would be more beneficial than what I could learn in a dozen hours online. Still, the issue isn't really about the content of the videos watched. It's simply about the extremity in how often and how much of them we watch. If I honestly want to get better at golf, why not do so in the most efficient way possible?

Now trade watching golf videos with simply posting one post on Instagram. Having seen first hand throughout this book how posting for the sake of likes and comments offers us no real value or aligns us with finding our true identities and purposes, we can easily conclude that spending so much time posting one post on Instagram is not only inefficient and wasteful, it can be harmful. It detracts from time spent actually making the most of our lives.

It also becomes an easy scapegoat to blame instead of working on the parts of our lives that *need* to be addressed. If you're unhappy with your job or relationship, don't complain if you're also wasting precious time on social media, doing things that not only distract you from your job and relationship goals but actively impede your achievement of those goals. We human beings are master avoiders. When we don't want to deal with something, we procrastinate in the most creative of ways. But social media? That's a pretty boring way. If you're going to procrastinate at all, at least make it time well spent: outside in a park, bonding with a friend at happy hour, or baking a pie just for the joy of baking. Procrastinating with an activity that ultimately just makes you feel worse about yourself is frankly a form of self-abuse.

The power of distraction...

There's a reason why the scenescape of a group of people all staring at their screens so easily likens us to *zombies*. When zombies are on the move, they've got tunnel vision on only one thing: eating brains! When we're glued to our phones, we've also got only one thing on our minds: distracting brains! It's amazing what great lengths we'll go to just *not think*. You'd imagine there's nothing modern people hate more than being alone with their own thoughts. At least, that's how we act.

But what if zombies had full access to eating human brains 24/7? They'd live how we live with social media: tunnel vision 24/7. We have access to distraction at our fingertips, whenever we want it. And that distraction is *endless*. We spend 15 minutes scrolling Instagram or Facebook, take a break for merely two minutes, and then come back to *another* 15 minutes worth of brand new content. We can never catch up with all the distraction. This means we never have to face the stillness of our own thoughts alone. How could this be affecting us psychologically?

A July 2015 Gallup study polling 15,747 adult smartphone users found that half check their phone a few times an hour (41%) or every few minutes (11%). When they focused on only 18 to 29-year-old smartphone users, those figures increased to 51% checking a few times an hour and 22% checking every few minutes.[57]

To make matters worse, it may not be a coincidence that the number of diagnoses of attention deficit disorder (ADHD or ADD) in the United States skyrocketed 43 percent between 2003 and 2011, totalling the number of American children with ADHD at nearly 6 million, according to 2015 statistics from the Center for Disease Control and Prevention.[58] In fact, many are afraid that our growing reliance on technology and addiction to screens may be a *cause* of our rising ADHD/ADD numbers.

Killing time or killing productivity?

According to Inc.com, "It's estimated that the average American spends nearly one quarter of their work day browsing social media for non-work related activities."[59] Sure, addiction to productivity—the pressure to be "busy" at all times—is another problem in itself. But let's assume

---

57   Larry D. Rosen, "This Is the Real Reason You Can't Stop Checking Your Phone," PsychologyToday.com, accessed June 2, 2018,https://www.psy-chologytoday.com/us/blog/rewired-the-psychology-technology/201507/is-the-real-reason-you-cant-stop-checking-your-phone.

58   "ADHD, By The Numbers," ADDitudemag.com, accessed June 9, 2018, https://www.additudemag.com/the-statistics-of-adhd/.

59   John Boitnott, "Social Media Addiction: The Productivity Killer," Inc. com, accessed April 24, 2018, https://www.inc.com/john-boitnott/so-cial-media-addiction-the-productivity-killer.html.

you have a healthy relationship with productivity; you only work during the workday. Outside of those hours, you lead a balanced life spending time with family and friends and doing the things you love to do. If that's your life, but then you also spend a full quarter of your workday on social media, wouldn't you call that a waste of productivity?

But productivity doesn't only exist in the workplace. For many of us, our day jobs are not what our greatest passions are. Those passions and goals exist outside of our nine to five job. So if social media is affecting productivity, isn't it affecting that productivity too? We spend so much time on our phones each day that it is physically impossible to have time for work, school, exercise, relationships, hobbies, and basic self care unless you only need four hours of sleep per night. If you've figured out how to balance it all, then *you* should write a book because you'd make millions!

Neuroscientists say there's no such thing as multitasking.

Our brains are "not wired to multitask well... When people think they're multitasking, they're actually just switching from one task to another very rapidly. And every time they do, there's a cognitive cost in doing so," says Earl Miller, an MIT neuroscientist and one of the world's experts on divided attention. So when we're checking Instagram while writing up an important presentation while also listening to an informative podcast about which cryptocurrency we should be investing in, we're actually not multitasking at all; we're just making less progress than we would in a bunch of tasks than we would if we focused on one task at a time. Miller added, "People can't do [multitasking] very well, and when they say they can, they're deluding themselves."

As award-winning scientist and teacher Daniel J. Levitin says in his bestseller, "We're not actually keeping a lot of balls in the air like an expert juggler; we're more like a bad amateur plate spinner, frantically switching from one task to another, ignoring the one that is not right in front of us, but worried it will come crashing down any minute."[60]

Multitasking creates a surge of the stress hormone cortisol as well as the fight-or-flight hormone adrenaline, which can overstimulate your brain, causing mental fog or scrambled thinking. Multitasking also creates a dopamine-addiction feedback loop, literally *rewarding* the brain for losing focus and searching for external stimulation constantly—rewarding bad behaviour and cementing bad habits. What's even crazier is that the prefrontal cortex is the region we need in order to stay on task, but it also has something called a novelty bias—a tendency to get easily distracted by any metaphorical shiny, new object.[61] Seriously?! This means the more we check our Facebook

60   Daniel J. Levitin, *The Organized Mind: Thinking Straight in the Age of Information Overload,* New York, NY: Dutton, 2016.

61   Daniel J. Levitin, *The Organized Mind: Thinking Straight in the Age of Information Overload,* New York, NY: Dutton, 2016.

feeds or scroll through Instagram, we light up the reward-seeking centers of the brain, training the brain to interpret this distraction as *good* and taking us away from the task at hand.

In fact, it's gotten to the point that simply having social media on the mind—feeling the *need* to check a notification waiting for us—can also poorly affect our cognitive performance. According to the research of Glenn Wilson, a former visiting professor of psychology at Gresham College, London, trying to concentrate on a task while having an email sitting unread in your inbox can reduce your effective IQ by 10 points.[62] The mere expectation of a dopamine surge caused by checking social media is enough to literally make us *dumber.* Wilson's research also revealed that even the significant cognitive losses of smoking pot pale in comparison to the cognitive losses from multitasking.

Part of the reason multitasking could be responsible for brain fog and scramble thinking is because the information "learned" while multitasking actually is filed into the wrong part of the brain, according to Russ Poldrack, a neuroscientist at Stanford.[63] For example, if students do homework and watch YouTube videos at the same time, the information from their schoolwork goes into the striatum, a region specialised for storing new procedures and skills. Without the distraction of YouTube,

---

62   Daniel J. Levitin, *The Organized Mind: Thinking Straight in the Age of Information Overload,* New York, NY: Dutton, 2016.

63   Daniel J. Levitin, *The Organized Mind: Thinking Straight in the Age of Information Overload,* New York, NY: Dutton, 2016.

the information goes into the hippocampus, the region for facts and ideas, organised in a highly logical and effective way.

So. If "multitasking" (if you still believe that's possible) is this harmful for us, imagine how much social media is contributing to that multitasking. We check Facebook while we work, we comment on Instagram while having a conversation with someone, we swipe through filter after filter for that selfie of us at that museum *while* we're still touring the museum, trying to learn something. In fact, I'd argue people mostly go on social media when they're also busy with something else. Why? Because they're searching for distraction from that other thing, whether they're aware of it or not. Nobody schedules out time to go on Facebook. Nobody pencils in "Instagram" in their calendar, where they can devote their undivided attention to randomly liking countless pictures. The very culture of social media is built upon multitasking. It's just *what you do* while you're doing something else too.

Conclusion

"Everyone wants to change, but no one is
willing to do anything differently."

– Eugene Burger

Do you feel inspired? You should. Rather than mourning your relationship with social media, remember: social media itself is not the problem—*we* are! And if there is ONE thing that is in our control to change, it is *ourselves.* If you want to go ahead and quit social media altogether, great! If you do not, you don't have to! You're now gaining self-awareness about your relationship with social media, and that should help guide you towards what is best for you.

Chances are: you are bored.

More and more people are living a purposeless life, waking up every morning wondering what they are on earth for, dreading Mondays, celebrating Fridays, living for the weekends and holidays, only to drop into a borderline depression come Monday again, praying for the end of the week all over again. It sounds silly, but even the fact that wishing people "Happy Friday" became commonplace a few years ago is a bit alarming to me. We might as well be saying, "Happy Friday—your week sucks so badly that we must celebrate the end of it!" over and over and over again. I don't know about you, but I honestly find this really sad, considering that most people spend most of their time at work, and most of them do not love their jobs. That's depressing. You'd think that people who dislike their jobs would make an extra effort to do things they truly love outside of work, but guess what: they don't. There aren't enough hours in the day, and most of us expend our energy on the work we don't enjoy before we even get a chance to do what we *do* enjoy. If you don't have anything going on in your life that excites you, that *isn't* limited to partying on the weekends, watching TV, or just spend countless hours online, then you've got a massive problem. If there's nothing you love to do that can change your state of mind and put a smile on your face when you're having a bad day, then you're missing out.

Too many of us rely on social media to fill that void. But if we rely on it to do that, then that void is *never* going to be filled. If anything, as we now know, the more we use social media as a substitute for things that provide real meaning, the more the void widens—the less we feel confident, happy, connected, belonging, fulfilled, purposeful. And that traps us in a nasty cycle.

So. Not counting social media... Have you ever been so genuinely interested in doing something that it's consumed you completely? That you went hours without checking your phone or days without posting anything online? If you have, then you've known joy. It's different from the rush of joy—dopamine—we get when a notification lights up our phone. The latter appeals to nothing more than a pathway transmission in our brain that we're physiologically trained to crave and seek out, like a sugar rush or an adrenaline rush. The joy you feel when you're consumed by a person, a project, a story—that joy is more stable and lasting. It's not an empty-caloried sugary treat that satisfies you for no more than two seconds. Rather, it's a feast for your soul, something to fuel and nourish you for long after.

Chase that. Maybe you've always wanted to try something, go somewhere, learn a language, play an instrument, reconnect with something you used to love doing as a child, but then let go of for some reason. And if you don't know what that thing is, then *look for it*. It's out there. The fact that you don't know what it is yet is just further evidence that you're wasting time on things that are not serving and nourishing you. When you have found your purpose, that fuel that drives you, that interest that feels like your life force, social media naturally loses its grasp on you.

And maybe that thing that drives you isn't a thing at all—maybe it's a person or many people. Invest your time and energy in people, because that will always reap gold for you. Give yourself to people with whom you can create something, share your secrets, unload your burdens, exchange ideas, travel the world. That person who randomly liked your post while sitting on the toilet is not going to change anything at all in your life. But your close friends and family will.

So I challenge you: make a list of things, people, places that interest you. Then choose your number one interest on that list. Then chase it.

Why do you share what you share? For whom? And how often?

I've said it many times throughout this book: at the end of the day, social media itself isn't really the issue. Problems arise only when your behaviour surrounding social media negatively impacts your life or the lives around you. The question always worth asking then is: Are you using it or is it using you?

We know that the whole point of social media is essentially sharing. But the questions that determine whether or not our relationship with social media is healthy are: why do we share what we share? How often do we share it? And for whom do we share it? Try to be as neutral and objective as possible and ask yourself those simple questions "Why? How often? And for whom?" The question lingering beneath these questions is: "Am I really posting for myself or am I posting with others' reactions and opinions in mind?" If we're having trouble determining an answer here, this question makes it easier: "If I share this and no one likes it or comments on it, will

I still be happy with my post or will I feel bad in some way or another?"

The Golden Advice.

If you could only take with you two things from this book, let them be these:

1. Never compare your inside with someone else's outside! That doesn't just go for social media. In general, this is one of the biggest mistakes people unconsciously make and end up feeling like crap. Other people will NEVER be you. You will NEVER be them. You and any other person are different; you have different paths, upbringings, values, talents, hobbies, knowledge, the list goes on. It doesn't make sense to compare yourself with anyone except someone who has an exact copy of your life experiences and genetic make up. But... no such person exists. Comparing ourselves to each other is like a fish looking at a bird and wishing it could fly and then a bird looking at the fish and envying its ability to breathe underwater.

2. Unless your social media profile is your business or you are a brand yourself, likes and online attention mean absolutely F*CK ALL. We are spending too much precious time in our lives trying to feel things—attractive, valued, important, connected—through

apps and more often than not, from people who don't know us and probably don't really care about us. And even if they DID care, that is still a far cry from their like on our post filling that huge void in our lives.

Where do we go from here?

Without awareness first, we can't change things. You have that awareness now. So what do you do with it? There is rarely one-size-fits-all when it comes to strategies and that is why I haven't even mentioned strategies until now… because strategies deserve an entire book themselves. This book isn't a self-help book to give you a detailed plan on how to turn your life around. It *is* a book to open your eyes to the possibility that you *can* turn your life around… in a way you likely never considered. I only brushed the surface here in order to raise awareness. I advise you to do some research and soul-searching yourself and see what you find. Your behaviour on social media is likely masking *something* that you don't want to face… so what is it? And if you find researching by yourself isn't enough, I encourage you to seek out the help of a specialist! After all, when something is broken in your car, you see a mechanic. When something is broken in you, you go see someone too. Seeing a coach, therapist, or specialist doesn't mean something is wrong with you. On the contrary, it means you're human like all of us and you're evolved and self-aware enough to admit it! It's the 21st century—help is out there so take advantage of it!

Nonetheless, I do have a few concrete tips for what I think you should do moving forward. Here they are.

1) Deep clean!

If you realise you've been posting shit or that your posts do not accurately reflect who you really are or who you'd like to be, if you realise the accounts you follow make you feel like crap or your own followers don't follow you for the right reasons, CLEAN UP YOUR ACCOUNTS. Consider it a virtual spring cleaning! You know when you go through your closet or your entire house and make a giveaway pile of the things you no longer use, don't need, remind you of people or experiences you want to let go of... and then you feel so much lighter? You end up feeling more free. Well, do the same with your social media accounts and trust me, it will feel the same. Toxic people? GONE. Pictures, videos, comments that do not really represent who you really are and how you want to be perceived and remembered? GONE. People whom you don't know and add no value to your life? GONE. Accounts you once followed as a singleton that now distract from your happy, healthy relationship you're now in? GONE. Accounts that realistically make you feel like shit because they create a false sense of reality or make you compare yourself to an unreal standard? GONE, GONE, GONE! Remember: you want to be real, not fake! Quality is much better than quantity! Time to upload the new version of yourself.

2) Beware of the halfway point.

If you've made up your mind to make a positive change in your life, just be aware of the halfway point; it is often where people give up and essentially go back to the exact same place they were trying to leave—or they retreat to somewhere even worse. Why do we do this? Because even if we know where we were wasn't good for us or helpful, at least it is known territory. The unknown always tends to be much scarier to us than the known. For example, no longer posting selfies to get the validation we need can feel a bit lonely at first. We might feel a bit down and see this as a negative outcome... when in fact, it's actually just a challenge we need to get through *before* we reap all the positive benefits. So many people take the necessary steps, start the journey, feel better, feel strong, and feel certain they are on the right path until they hit a little speed bump. Remind yourself that this journey happens one step at a time, through ups and downs, good and bad. Taking a stand for what you want is brave and you need to trust that it's worth it. It might be easier in the short term to stay where you are, but it's much easier in the long term to live the rest of your life somewhere much, much better.

3) Treat your social media like a personal journal.

We know social media is about sharing. As long as we don't hinge our self-worth on what *results* from that sharing, then our relationship with social media is healthy. A good way to cultivate this relationship is by treating social media as if it's a personal journal or photo album. I consider it like I would a corkboard in my house where I would pin cool stuff, images that make me happy or proud, memories that make me smile. I treat it as something that supports my values and goals. If a stranger looked at it, I'd want him or her to be able to describe the person I truly am in a few words—not some fake alter ego people think I am.

4) Give your phone (and thumbs) a rest!

Sure, you use your phone for things beside social media, but honestly, taking a break from screen time no matter what's on the screen is beneficial. Here's how to cut down on that screen time so that when you *are* looking at your phone, you're making it count.

Turn of some (or all!) social media notifications. By turning off your notifications you're essentially saving yourself from being sucked back online and ruining whatever progress you're making. A fun bonus? By having them off, when you do go and check them, what you find will always feel fun because it'll be an unexpected surprise.

Move the social media apps icons off your home screen to another page or into an apps folder. I have personally done this and I find that whenever I use my phone, those shiny and tempting app icons are not right there in my face, waiting to be pressed. Like many of you, I used to find myself going on social media out of boredom, just to randomly scroll and kill time. Since doing this, I have honestly reduced my social media visits from dozens of times a day to a small handful.

Monitor and limit your time on social media by "scheduling" time in your day specifically for checking, browsing, and posting on social media. And here's the key: do not go on social media outside of that scheduled time. Here are some ideas for example: do not check social media within the first hour of being awake, don't check it during working hours, and don't check an hour before bed so you have a chance to wind down. Maybe schedule mini-vacations away from social media where you don't check them for a full day or a full week. Watch what happens—your life will blossom in ways you didn't know possible. When you're with family or friends, leave your phone switched off, at home, in another room, or in your bag. You could even download an app (like Offtime, Moment, Breakfree or many others) that monitor how long you spend on social media, and blocks certain apps at certain times.

Social media is a learned behaviour and any learned behaviour can be unlearned.

However, remember that it is crucial to maintain balance. When you get rid of something, replace it with something beneficial. Don't trade one addiction for another. For example, avoiding social media when you first wake up, but wallowing over celebrity news on the internet instead isn't much of a step up. Instead, focus on creating a life you wake up *buzzing* to live. We create new habits by repetition. Your best life can be your new habit that you create. I have full faith in you!

Whether you identify with some or many points in this book, or you recognise the issues raised in people close to you, your openness and willingness to change is admirable. There's a part of all of us that is aware of the dangers of our current behaviour.

Being aware of the negative effects of social media, I now approach boredom differently. I'd rather wait on a park bench and simply mindlessly watch the world around me than watch my phone. There is always something to learn in simply being—not needing distraction to keep you from being alone with yourself.

Try being alone with yourself. Listen to your thoughts. Listen to your fears. Listen to your desires. When you're actually listening and not distracting, you give yourself space to actually register the problems in your life so you can give yourself an actual shot at fixing them.

When you close this book, don't feel pressure to delete all your social media apps cold turkey. I'm not sure the other extreme is better than the one most of us lean towards. Simple awareness of where you are on that scale of extremes is enough to initiate change. Being aware of how social media affects you negatively is a huge step towards helping yourself. Awareness opens the door to conscious decision-making—something most of us do not practice when it comes to social media. Our phones are like an extra limb, and we've grown so used to them that our interaction with them is habitual, mindless, and unconscious. But as we've seen, unconscious and subconscious action makes as much of a difference in our lives (if not more) than conscious action. So by making as much of your action as *conscious* as you can, you shine light on any confusion you have in your life simply by acknowledging the confusion. I want to give you the best shot at the life you truly dream of for yourself. But only you can give yourself that shot.

> "I'm not telling you it is going to be easy—I'm telling you it's going to be worth it."
>
> – Arthur L. Williams, Jr.

Acknowledgements

Once they have been hurt one too many times, too many people unfortunately close their door to protect themselves from getting hurt again. More often than not, this works; they are now water tight and well "protected." However, though this keeps the crap from coming in, it also keeps the good things from coming in. That closed door keeps out good people, good opportunities, miracles and blessings. Then these people are left with nothing but the bitter taste of whatever hurt them before they closed the door, while simultaneously wondering why nothing new, good, or fun ever comes their way. Open your door, and trust me, it will. Of course some crap will come in too, but the key is learning how to process and dispose of the crap in a healthy way instead of just avoiding it at all costs. If you spend your life hiding, you sacrifice *living*. Trust the process and in the end, you'll end up with more good in your life than bad.

I live my life with an open door policy. My door has always been open, anyone and everything could walk in, at anytime, for any reason. God knows I've had my fair share of things that proved to be not so positive, but even considering that, I can honestly say that far more positive things and people have come into my life than negative.

So much so that I don't even remember the bad because I've let it go. I am who I am today, done what I've done, and learned what I've learned thanks to PEOPLE... a lot of them. I have been extremely lucky with great influences and a lot of help along the way.

Considering the success of my entire life, journey, and this book, I have too many people to thank for their help, patience, guidance and much more, so I do apologise if I miss anyone. I am grateful to you regardless of whether your name is written here.

The first person I would like to thank has to be my dad, Alain. He doesn't realise the immense, positive impact he has had on my life and how I think. He instilled in me such powerful curiosity and tools to be an effective observer, and I believe I am a coach and "philosopher" because of him. That means this book would not exist without him. Thank you to my mum, Danielle, for all her patience and support, even when I was being a little shit! Thanks to my step mum, Veronique, who basically teamed up with my dad in cultivating that curiosity in me and encouraging me down this path. I must thank my brother, Matthias, who has been at my side through thousands of defining experiences. Thanks to my sisters, Roxane, Evane, and Orane, who challenged my ideas and theories constantly, and, therefore pushed me to keep looking deeper and deeper.

I would like to thank my two best friends, Ramzan and Vijay, who are brothers to me. They've had my back, pushed me forward, listened and supported me for many years. Of course we will never know what would have happened if they didn't, but holy cow they've saved my skin many times!

Thanks to Traci, Karim, Freddie and Bernard. These four people are the MAIN reason why I eventually believed in myself enough to become a coach. I found courage in them to write this book. Thank you so much, guys. You honestly are inspirations!

I would like to thank my good friend, Rachael, who for years has been a very good listener and adviser. It is a gift to have a really good female friend, always there to offer a different set of ideas, perspectives, and experiences.

Massive thank you to Gary, Bill, and Virginie. I cannot describe how patient, helpful, resourceful and so much more they have been.

More thanks to Emily Crook Art for the book cover. Thank you to Jill, Sue, James and Gail for assisting with the logistic around the book. Thank you for being part of this journey, for your time, help, advice, and encouragement.

Finally I would like to thank my editor, Desirée. Earlier I mentioned my open door policy and just trusting the journey. When I was looking for an editor, the ONLY person that I ended up reaching out to was Desirée. I had an instant gut feeling that she was the one who'd turn this book from good to great. God knows it has been loads of work and I certainly wasn't the easiest client, but she was patient, extremely helpful, and literally worked magic. Thank you!

Bibliography

Adams, Mike. "Is Social Media As Addictive As Cocaine?" High Times. Accessed June
11, 2018. https://hightimes.com/news/social-media-addictive-cocaine/.

"ADHD, By The Numbers." ADDitudemag.com. Accessed June 9, 2018. https://www.additudemag.com/the-statistics-of-adhd/.

Asano, Evan. "How Much Time Do People Spend on Social Media?"

SocialMediaToday.com. Accessed June 1, 2018. https://www.socialmediatoday.com/marketing/how-much-time-do-people-spend-social-media-infographic.

Aslam, Salman. "Facebook by the Numbers: Stats, Demographics & Fun Facts."

Omnicore. Accessed June 7, 2018. https://www.omnicoreagency.com/facebook-statistics/.— "Instagram by the Numbers: Stats, Demographics & Fun Facts."

Omnicore. Accessed June 7, 2018. https://www.omnicoreagency.com/instagram-statistics/.

— "Snapchat by the Numbers: Stats, Demographics & Fun Facts."

Omnicore. Accessed May 23, 2018. https://www.omnicoreagency.com/snapchat-statistics/.

— "YouTube by the Numbers: Stats, Demographics & Fun

Facts." Omnicore. Accessed May 23, 2018. https://www. omnicoreagency.com/youtube-statistics/.

Balakrishnan, M.D., J. Griffiths. Int J Ment Health Addiction (2018) 16: 722. Accessed June 6, 2018. https://doi. org/10.1007/s11469-017-9844-x.

Bartiromo, Michael. "'Cocaine babe' tells court she smuggled drugs for 'likes and attention' on Instagram." Fox News. Accessed May 2, 2018. http://www.foxnews.com/ travel/2018/03/22/cocaine-babe-tells-court-smuggled-drugs-for-likes-and-attention-on-instagram.html.

Bessant, Claire. "Do parents share too many pictures of their child online?" International Business Times. Accessed May 24, 2018. https://www.ibtimes.co.uk/do-parents-share-too-many-pictures-their-children-online-1640174.

Best, Shivali. "Liking someone's Instagram post is now seen as 'micro-cheating' and can DESTROY your marriage." MSN. com. Accessed June 1, 2018. https://www.msn.com/en-gb/ lifestyle/family-relationships/liking-someones-instagram-post-is-now-seen-as-micro-cheating-and-can-destroy-your-marriage/ar-AAuImxv.

Boitnott, John. "Social Media Addiction: The Productivity Killer." Inc.com. Accessed April 24, 2018. https://www. inc.com/john-boitnott/social-media-addiction-the-productivity-killer.html.

Burke, Kenneth. "How Much Time Do People Spend on Their Mobile Phones in 2018?" Textrequest.com. Accessed May 23, 2018. https://www.textrequest.com/blog/how-much-time-people-spend-mobile-phones-2017/.

Castillo, Juan. "25 Shocking Facts About Porn You Probably Didn't Know." List25.com. Accessed June 1, 2018. https:// list25.com/25-shocking-facts-about-porn/.

Donnelly, Gordon. "75 Super-Useful Facebook Statistics for 2018." Wordstream. Accessed May 20, 2018. https://www.wordstream.com/blog/ws/2017/11/07/facebook-statistics.

Dreher, Diane. "Why Are Today's College Students So Emotionally Fragile?"

Psychology Today. Accessed June 1, 2018. https://www.psychologytoday.com/us/blog/your-personal-renaissance/201508/why-are-today-s-college-students-so-emotionally-fragile.

Egan, Matt. "Facebook and Amazon hit $500 Billion Milestone." Money.CNN.com.

Accessed May 23, 2018. http://money.cnn.com/2017/07/27/investing/facebook-amazon-500-billion-bezos-zuckerberg/index.html.

Firestone, Lisa. "Self-Esteem Versus Narcissism." Psychology Today. Accessed June 1, 2018. https://www.psychologytoday.com/us/blog/compassion-matters/201206/self-esteem-versus-narcissism.

Gajanan, Mahita. "Young women on Instagram and self-esteem: 'I absolutely feel insecure.'" The Guardian. Accessed June 1, 2018. https://www.theguardian.com/media/2015/nov/04/instagram-young-women-self-esteem-essena-oneill.

Garcia-Navarro, Lulu. "The Risk Of Teen Depression And Suicide Is Linked To Smartphone Use, Study Says." NPR. Accessed May 23, 2018. https://www.npr.org/2017/12/17/571443683/the-call-in-teens-and-depression.

Gould-Bourn, James. "This Is How Male Body Ideals Have Changed Over Time." BoredPanda.com. Accessed June 23, 2018. https://www.boredpanda.com/male-body-ideals-throughout-time/.

Granet, Rebecca. "Living In Live Time: Social Media's Impact On Girls." CBS New York. Accessed May 24, 2018. http://newyork.cbslocal.com/2016/09/19/social-media-use-teens/.

"Have we created unsocial media?" Kaspersky Lab Daily. Accessed May 24, 2018. https://usa.kaspersky.com/blog/digital-depression/10643/.

Hebblethwaite, Colm. "The average person has 7 social media accounts." Marketing Tech News. Accessed June 1, 2018. https://www.marketingtechnews.net/news/2017/nov/17average-person-has-7-social-media-accounts/.

Highfield, Roger. "Microwave Sparked Obesity Epidemic." The Telegraph. Accessed May 23, 2018. https://www.telegraph.co.uk/news/uknews/1553734/Microwave-sparked-obesity-epidemic.html.

"How Much Time Do We Spend on Social Media?" Mediakix.com. Accessed May 20, 2018. http://mediakix.com/2016/12/how-much-time-is-spent-on-social-media-lifetime/#gs.jryzpdk.

Hunt, Elle. "Essena O'Neill quits Instagram claiming social media 'is not real life.'" The Guardian. Accessed June 1, 2018. https://www.theguardian.com/media/2015/nov/03/instagram-star-essena-oneill-quits-2d-life-to-reveal-true-story-behind-images.

"Instagram is Worth Over $100 Billion." Mediakix. Accessed May 23, 2018. http://mediakix.com/2017/12/how-much-is-instagram-worth-market-cap/#gs.=Ik7B3E.

James, Georgia. "Research Suggests All Men Watch Pornography." Huffington Post. Accessed June 1, 2018. https://www.huffingtonpost.co.uk/2011/08/18/research-suggests-all-men-watch-pornography_n_930349.html?guccounter=1.

Lamba, Hemank and Varun Bharadhwaj, Mayank Vachher, Divyansh Agarwal, Megha Arora, Ponnurangam Kumaraguru. "Me, Myself and My Killfie: Characterizing and Preventing Selfie Deaths." Accessed June 1, 2018. https://arxiv.org/pdf/1611.01911v2.pdf.

Lenhart, A., and K. Purcell, A. Smith, K. Zickur. "Social Media and Young Adults." Washington, DC: Pew Research Center; 2010. Accessed May 24, 2018. http://pewinternet. org/Reports/2010/Social-Media-and-Young-Adults.aspx.

Lehnardt, Karin. "81 Shocking Facts about Pornography." Fact Retriever. Accessed June

1, 2018. https://www.factretriever.com/pornography-facts.

Levitin, Daniel J. *The Organized Mind: Thinking Straight in the Age of Information Overload,* New York, NY: Dutton, 2016.

Lister, Mary. "33 Mind-Boggling Instagram Stats & Facts for 2018." Accessed May 23, 2018. https://www.wordstream. com/blog/ws/2017/04/20/instagram-statistics.

"Lying Less Linked to Better Health, New Research Finds." American Psychological Association. Accessed June 1, 2018. http://www.apa.org/news/press/releases/2012/08/ lying-less.aspx.

Macmillan, Amanda. "Millennials Who Use More Social Media Sites Have Higher Depression, Anxiety." Health. com. Accessed May 21, 2018. http://www.health.com/ depression/multiple-social-media-sites-depression-anxiety.

Mozes, Alan. "The Complex Link Between Social Media and Depression." Health.com. Accessed May 21, 2018. http:// www.health.com/depression/could-lots-of-time-spent-on-social-media-be-tied-to-depression.

"Online Abuse Facts & Statistics." NSPCC.org. Accessed May

24, 2018. https://www.nspcc.org.uk/preventing-abuse/child-abuse-and-neglect/online-abuse/facts-statistics/.

Orzel, Chad. "Particles and Waves; The Central Mystery of Quantum Mechanics." TEDEd video, 4:52. Accessed May 2, 2018. https://ed.ted.com/lessons/particles-and-waves-the-central-mystery-of-quantum-mechanics-chad-orzel.

Quinn, Calder and Brad Rickman. "Selfies vs. Shark Attacks: Which Are More Deadly for Travelers?" Condé Nast Traveler. Accessed June 1, 2018. https://www.cntraveler.com/stories/2015-09-15/selfies-vs-shark-attacks-which-is-more-deadly-for-travelers?tw=social.

"Rise in Teen Suicide Connected to Social Media Popularity: Study." NYPost.com. Accessed May 24, 2018. https://nypost.com/2017/11/14/rise-in-teen-suicide-connected-to-social-media-popularity-study/.

Robehmed, Natalie. "How Kim Kardashian West Bounced Back To $45.5 Million--And A New Cosmetics Company." Forbes. Accessed May 20, 2018. https://www.forbes.com/sites/natalierobehmed/2017/06/13/how-kim-kardashian-west-bounced-back-to-45-5-million-and-a-new-cosmetics-company/.

Romm, Cari. "The Psychology of Oversharing Facebook Couples." The Atlantic. Accessed June 1, 2018. https://www.theatlantic.com/health/archive/2014/08/the-psychology-of-oversharing-facebook-couples/376112/.

Rosen, Larry D. "This Is the Real Reason You Can't Stop Checking Your Phone." PsychologyToday.com. Accessed June 2, 2018. https://www.psychologytoday.com/us/blog/rewired-the-psychology-technology/201507/is-the-real-reason-you-cant-stop-checking-your-phone.

Ross, Carolyn. "Overexposed and Under-Prepared: The Effects

of Early Exposure to Sexual Content." Psychology Today. Accessed May 24, 2018. https://www.psychologytoday.com/us/blog/real-healing/201208/overexposed-and-under-prepared-the-effects-early-exposure-sexual-content.

"Sexualisation of Young People in the Media." Zero Tolerance. Accessed May 2, 2018. http://www.zerotolerance.org.uk/sites/www.zerotolerance.org.uk/files/files/SexualisationBriefing_ForDownloadV1.pdf.

Shemenski, Jay. "The Future of Social Media is Mobile. Are You Ready?" Simplymeasured.com. Accessed May 23, 2018. https://simplymeasured.com/blog/the-future-of-social-media-is-mobile-are-you-ready/.

Silva, Clarissa. "Social Media's Impact on Self Esteem." HuffPost. Accessed May 24, 2018. https://www.huffingtonpost.com/entry/social-medias-impact-on-self-esteem_us_58ade038e4b0d818c4f0a4e4.

Smith, Kit. "39 Fascinating and Incredible YouTube Statistics." Brandwatch.com. Accessed May 23, 2018. https://www.brandwatch.com/blog/39-youtube-stats/.

Stack, Steven and Ira Wasserman and Roger Kern. "Adult Social Bonds and Use of Internet Pornography," Social Science Quarterly 85, (2004): 75-88.

"Subliminal Messages Research." Deeptrancenow.com. Accessed May 22, 2018. http://www.deeptrancenow.com/subliminal_messages.htm.

"The Impact of Social Media Use on Social Skills." Newyorkbehavioralhealth.com. Accessed May 24, 2018. http://newyorkbehavioralhealth.com/the-impact-of-social-media-use-on-social-skills.

"These 8 Social Media Addiction Statistics Show Where We're Spending Our Time." Mediakix. Accessed May 22, 2018.

http://mediakix.com/2018/04/social-media-addiction-statistics/#gs.0MLRSSk.

Zweig, David. "Why We Should Take Fewer Pictures of Our Children." The New York Times. Accessed May 24, 2018. https://parenting.blogs.nytimes.com/2012/10/12/why-we-should-take-fewer-pictures-of-our-children/.